MANIPULATION, DOMINATION AND CONTROL

Manipulation, Domination and Control

PRINCE YINKA OYEKAN

KINGSWAY PUBLICATIONS
EASTBOURNE

ISBN 0 85476 898 X

Published by
KINGSWAY PUBLICATIONS
Lottbridge Drove, Eastbourne, BN23 6NT, England.
Email: books@kingsway.co.uk

Designed and produced for the publishers by
Bookprint Creative Services, P.O. Box 827, BN21 3YJ, England.
Printed in Great Britain.

Contents

Foreword

One of the greatest hindrances to God's purpose for his church is the amount of manipulation, domination and control that exists among some Christians. Sometimes leaders dominate and control their congregations instead of leading them sensitively in the Spirit. At other times strong-willed members manipulate their leaders through a kind of spiritual blackmail.

There are too many who try to manipulate their fellow Christians to love them, take notice of them, and lavish time upon them. They do this by appealing to their own weakness, need or history of rejection. There are even 'counsellors' who dominate the weak and seek to control them.

Does this sound depressing? Well, it states the need for this book. It is sad that the need is so widespread. However, the gospel is about good news! The good news is that believers in Jesus Christ do not need to manipulate, dominate or control others. Neither do they need to allow themselves to be manipulated or to remain under anyone's domination and control.

This book will show you how to exercise faith in Jesus to overcome in any of these situations. It will help you if you minister to others to see how these problems can be addressed in their lives. It will also open your eyes to understand some of the dynamics that are operating in your relationships and possibly in the congregation to which you belong. Whatever your situation, the Lord wants you to have good, healthy relationships with others based on loving one another with the same love with which he loves you.

Colin Urquhart

Introduction

It hurts to see loved ones being adversely influenced by other people. Have you ever felt frustrated as you have watched a friend become dominated by another individual and not known what to do about it? This book seeks to help Christians recognise and deal with various forms of domination and manipulation. In it I hope to help dominated individuals accept the reality of their position, and then to show them how, through the love of Christ, they can handle the person or people responsible for manipulating them. Additionally, the material in this book should help everyone who reads it determine whether or not they are dominators themselves. It is important that all Christians face the issue of domination not just because of the potential problems that can arise within their circle of friends, but also because of the resulting difficulties that an unchecked dominating personality can bring into church life.

As I have travelled around Britain pastors have shown great interest in the subject of this book. Many have testified that the effects of selfish manipulation can last for years and leave members of a congregation emotionally scarred. The scope of manipulation in the church has surprised me. As a consequence a chapter of this book is devoted specifically to that subject. While we try to clean up the world, it is important that we take care to clean up our own street, and before this our own house. Using people to achieve personal ends is wicked by any standard, but though such behaviour is to be expected among unbelievers, it is sad to find the same level of selfishness among believers.

In one church, for example, an extremely successful and wealthy Christian offered competent individuals from his local church a job in his company. Mandy, a highly qualified young lady, was one among a few who gratefully accepted his offer. On the surface it seemed quite a good opportunity. She was told that as long as she combined hard work with loyalty and faithfulness she would be adequately rewarded by the company. Her department undoubtedly worked very hard, as the whole company was profitable on the strength of their sales. But five years after joining the company her salary had only increased by two thousand pounds while the salaries of friends with comparable responsibilities and jobs in other companies had increased by ten thousand pounds. The company itself had enjoyed competitive profits over this period. In fact the company was doing so well that in a time of recession it was taking on new employees.

During this period Mandy was asked to train new and junior staff who were accountable to her. She was hurt to learn that these new and junior employees were being taken on at a salary significantly higher than she was earning herself. It was this that finally caused Mandy to face the facts. She and others in the church who had been given jobs were being used. Yet, despite this conclusion, she felt obliged to stay on not only because the businessman was a member of her church but also because he made them all feel indebted to him for giving them a job.

Though his manipulative method of employing Christians was recognised by others within the church, I was surprised that nobody had yet done anything about it. This Christian businessman was definitely not a man of integrity. I believe that if he had been properly discipled by other godly men his whole attitude to business would have been different: 'As iron sharpens iron, so one man sharpens another' (Proverbs 27:17).

Many of the other examples within this book are deeply challenging to everyday church life. Although most of the examples are easy to understand it will take courage and honesty to face some of the issues raised – it will also demand commitment to deal with them. To appreciate the severity and offence of domination, we need to realise that it is the individual's liberty that is being stolen. Without freedom, the human spirit feels crushed and limited: 'A cheerful heart is good medicine, but a crushed spirit dries up the bones' (Proverbs 17:22).

Looking at the extreme example of rape can help us understand the wickedness of ungodly repression. Rape is usually thought of as being a physical and emotional violation of an individual's 'will', but is in fact much more than that: it is a violation of an individual's spirit as well as an offence against their body and soul. Ultimately all forms of manipulation take away from an individual's physical, emotional or spiritual independence. Real freedom is the ability to embrace a course of action that pleases God, regardless of any attempt by others to hinder. 'It is for freedom that Christ has set us free. Stand firm, then, and do not let yourselves be burdened again by a yoke of slavery' (Galatians 5:1).

The elements responsible for bringing people under bondage come from the following main sources. First we will consider people who assert their own desires. I have divided this category of dominator into three chapters dealing with people who dominate, and why they dominate; domination in the church and its effects; and manipulation between family and friends. Then we will look at the desires that battle inside individuals, sometimes causing them to do or say things they know are wrong, followed by an investigation of domination by demonic forces that wage war against the saints. Finally, we will examine how to break free from the power of manipulation and domination, whatever the source.

Note: Names have been changed to protect the identity of individuals concerned.

1

People Who Dominate

People are one of the greatest single sources of domination or manipulation. At different points in time people will exercise varying amounts of power or authority over others. This will either be negative, unauthorised and ungodly, or positive, authorised and in line with the word of God.

Humankind's sphere of dominance

In his wisdom, God has determined exactly how much humankind should have under their dominion (Genesis 1:26). God made humans to be kings and rulers over all the works of his hand, and the psalmist says that God actually placed all his works under humanity's feet (Psalm 8:6). Thus humans have a right to exercise dominion over all the animals and creatures they interact with.

In God's original plan it is not stated that a human should have dominion over another human. The only time domination of others is acceptable, is when God has ordered it. To dominate or lord it over another person is therefore an attempt to extend your sphere of dominion over and against what God originally intended. Domination outside the express will of God could also be termed rebellion against God, as it is a seeking of power not given by God to man.

God himself treats all people even-handedly, causing his sun to rise on the evil and the good, sending his rain on both the righteous and the unrighteous (Matthew 5:45). The impartiality of God is reflected in Jesus' teaching:

> But you are not to be called 'Rabbi', for you have only one Master and you are all brothers. And do not call anyone on earth 'father', for you have one Father, and he is in heaven. Nor are you to be called 'teacher', for you have one Teacher, the Christ. The greatest among you will be your servant. For whoever exalts himself will be humbled, and whoever humbles himself will be exalted. (Matthew 23:8–12)

Here Jesus exhorts his disciples to respect one another as close brothers, and to honour others by serving them. Indeed Christians were to be marked out not by their position but by their service.

Revealing the manipulator and the dominator

It is important to approach the following sections of this chapter with the right motivation. They will give attributes that will help you to identify the dominator or dominated person. Once we identify the symptoms revealing the manipulator or dominator, we need to make sure that we don't react against individuals we realise are dominators.

Instead of reacting we need to respond like Jesus would, confronting the issue while trying to help the person. In dealing with dominators or the dominated we must have love as our motivation – they are not objects to practise our particular ministries upon. Every effort must be made to ensure that we do not add to the emotional damage that may already have taken place. Since dominators usually find it difficult to accept that they have been manipulating, we need to be sure that we take counsel from other believers, and that we receive instruction from the word of God on how best to deal with any particular individual or circumstance.

Domination is not exercised in an emotionless vacuum: there are certain expectations preceding such an exercise. The dominator's feelings will be involved, either because he or she has something to gain, or because there is a desire to act in the subdued person's best interest. Thus the emotional reactions of strangers, friends and even family can sometimes help us to determine when and where manipulation is involved.

When an individual is working out of self-interest the following characteristics can indicate that domination is taking place. They do not represent domination where the individual is not acting out of negative emotional feelings such as hate, and has rightful authority to intervene, as in the case of a loving father imposing discipline on a naughty child.

1. *Possessive and obsessive*

Dominators and manipulators are both possessive. They jealously guard their sphere of control, and irrespective of how little influence they have upon another individual, they will put up some form of resistance in an attempt to maintain dominance. Where there is an obsessive need to dominate, dominators will engineer circumstances seeking to ensure that their sphere of power is difficult to erode.

A certain woman called May did just that. May immediately began to oversee the spiritual development of anyone converted, either as a result of her witnessing, or as a consequence of the witness of anyone already under her domination. One day a young man called Danny, converted through May's witnessing, received the baptism of the Holy Spirit. Before Danny was baptised in the Holy Spirit, he had struggled with sins from his past. These past sins had left him ineffective and powerless in his Christian life. Danny felt a hypocrite: on Sundays he would be at church doing the things he saw all his other Christian brothers and sisters doing, but during the week he lived a worldly lifestyle.

Eventually Danny decided to spend a week doing nothing but crying out to the Lord for the strength to walk honourably before him. He reasoned that if God could not help him to walk righteously, then no one else could. On the last day of that week his cry to the Lord was heard and he was filled with the Holy Spirit. Once baptised in the Holy Spirit his whole life started changing for the better. He found that the Scriptures, which had been so difficult to read, became exciting and began to build him up on the inside and strengthen his faith in God. Realising that he had been released from the sins that had bound him, he chose to devote his time to prayer and reading the Bible.

May was extremely threatened by Danny's new-found strength: she realised he was no longer dependent upon her. In an attempt to maintain her spiritual hold over Danny she told him that some of his new-found charismatic experiences were of the devil. Up to that point Danny had never had reason to doubt May and so accepted what she said. This resulted in his developing a dreadful fear of the devil. He concluded that when he called out to the Lord for help the devil responded and somehow got in before God could help.

One day Danny broke down and told some of his friends how afraid he had now become of Satan. His friends counselled him to reject what May had said. Danny did this and told May what he felt. He explained the fear and desperation her counsel had produced in him. May refused to acknowledge that she had been wrong. At first Danny could not understand why, but it later dawned on him that she found it impossible to receive any correction, small or large, from someone who had been brought to salvation through her witnessing. Everyone else believed that it was the Lord who was at work in this young man, but May could not accept that she was wrong and would not accept the testimony of anyone else about Danny.

Danny's case is not unique. All over the country there are many who have never stepped out in faith to do anything for God because they have been smothered by a spiritual parent. There is no room for a normal relationship with the dominator and manipulator. A degree of subservience is required. Once his or her grip on a person is broken, as in the case of Danny, the dominator will not enter any other kind of relationship. Dominators perceive the normal activity of growing up in faith and then breaking free from their spiritual apron strings as an act of betrayal. When things go wrong in the relationship, they attempt to justify their own position by placing most if not all of the blame on the once dominated individual.

Normally most people don't try to manipulate everyone they come into contact with. Rather, control is only attempted with certain individuals. One lady called Tanya had no problems relating to a group of female friends in her local fellowship. Tanya could share her problems with her circle of friends if another lady called Jane was absent. Jane enjoyed a healthy relationship with most of her other friends, but tried to mother Tanya. She felt that Tanya should appreciate her advice as weighty. A battle of wills would commence if Tanya refused to endorse Jane's advice.

Just as in the case of May, Jane's motherly instincts caused her to try to impose her advice on her friend. Like May, Jane found it difficult, and sometimes impossible, to accept that she was wrong once her advice had been given. Jane's possessiveness or obsessiveness ruined the possibility of a good relationship with Tanya.

2. *Coercive and violent*

The need to see others bow down to demands can result in the manipulator using ingenious methods to establish or maintain influence over a person. Consider the example of a spoilt child who wants something. Before he learns ingenious methods of acquiring what he wants, he displays a great deal of wilfulness sometimes expressed in tantrums. Of course a well-disciplined child soon learns that a screaming fit secures little more than a smack. The spoilt child, though, sometimes learns to bide his time until visitors are around. He has learned over a period of time that his parents will give in to his demands rather than be embarrassed. His ingenuity is shown in his ability to channel his wilfulness into methods he knows are going to work.

The grown-up manipulator too can be ingenious. Normally their behaviour pattern will have left them with a hardened conscience, so they have no qualms about taking advantage of another's circumstances. Placing demands or requests upon someone when they can't say no, is merely a means of getting their own way. This is the same principle that blackmailers use. Often we read or hear about people who have paid blackmailers thousands of pounds to keep them from releasing potentially embarrassing information. Blackmailers find out an individual's deepest secret and then use the information against their victim. They maintain their grip by intimidation, threatening to do something to embarrass or harm the victim if not obeyed or paid.

Clearly coercion has been shown to work – it makes people accept repression without much resistance. This is especially true where obedience has been secured through an initial massive show of force. We can all think of a country that has coupled brutal repression with continuous intimidation, thereby suppressing its people into adopting imposed styles and standards of living. The individual seeking to control may only need to use force once. Coercion is then maintained by the threat to use violence. Manipulators may exhibit aggressiveness as part of their character. The aggressiveness is usually but not always directed at the person the controller is trying to influence.

Take Susan, a young married woman. Susan was normally quite placid – a loveable character. Yet whenever she wanted her husband to do something that she knew he would not do willingly, she became aggressive. Rather than attempting to reason with her husband about the merits of her request, she resorted to aggression. It did not matter whom she displayed this aggression against, because she knew that her husband would be quickly subdued by her bad mood and, to pacify her, would give in to any requests she made. For Susan aggression was a vehicle through which she could manipulate her husband.

People being manipulated soon realise that they are being frustrated by the expectations of manipulators. The weight of these expectations before long generates behaviour that is in conflict with the personal desires of the manipulated person. Peter, for instance, attempted to frustrate Jesus from the way of the cross. He had recently confessed that Jesus was the Christ (Matthew 16:16), and the long-awaited Messiah of the Jewish people. But the idea that the Messiah was going to suffer was one he found hard to accept. This gave room for the devil to use him in an attempt to stop Jesus from going to the cross:

> From that time on Jesus began to explain to his disciples that he must go to Jerusalem and suffer many things at the hands of the elders, chief priests and teachers of the law, and that he must be killed and on the third day be raised to life. Peter took him aside and began to rebuke him. 'Never, Lord!' he said. 'This shall never happen to you!' Jesus turned and said to Peter, 'Get behind me, Satan! You are a stumbling-block to me; you do not have in mind the things of God, but the things of men.' Then Jesus said to his disciples, 'If anyone would come after me, he must deny himself and take up his cross and follow me.' (Matthew 16:21–4)

Now, it could be said that Peter was well meaning and that his expectations as a Jew caused him to reject the idea of a crucified Messiah. But Jesus had made it clear in his life and teaching that he always obeyed the express command of the Father. Like Peter, well-intentioned people may weigh us down with expectations, coming in the form of advice or direction contrary to what God has clearly said to us.

I especially remember one man. He had recently become a Christian, causing his wife to rejoice. She along with her close-knit group of friends had prayed for over five years for his conversion. But during this period of waiting they had also begun to plan what he should do once he became a Christian. When Tommy finally gave his life to the Lord, they began to condition him by telling him that he would make a good elder. They did not consider the pressure they were putting him under and began to weigh him down with their expectations. The result was that Tommy was being forced to act as if he were a much more mature Christian, yet he barely had a grasp of the most elementary doctrines of the faith. He had begun to live out the expectations placed upon him by others. Two years later I saw him again and found him totally backslidden. I shared the gospel with him and he repented and recommitted himself to Jesus. His wife also repented of what she had put him through. The expectations of friends can be a serious setback to the growth of an individual. But it can also be a serious blow to the growth of a church.

A pastor I knew was weighed down with conflicting desires from sizeable groups in the church. Two years previously he had been baptised in the Holy Spirit. Prior to this, the pastor had spent a decade preaching that this baptism in the Holy Spirit only ever happened at conversion. Great things began to happen in the church. Most of the elders visited a prominent Baptist church and were baptised in the Holy Spirit. The leadership as a whole began to have moving and intimate experiences of the Holy Spirit. Unfortunately a small but powerful minority in the fellowship opposed this new move of God. The pastor came under a great deal of pressure from all sides, receiving many complaints.

As a result he fell seriously ill. Both factions wrote to him detailing their expectations. Some hoped he would encourage prophesying in the church. Others wanted things to return to normal as soon as possible. Many of these made it clear that they were part of the original founding members and so in their view had a right to decide what direction the church ought to be heading in. Others demanded that the direction of the church should continue to change. Regardless of the sincerity of their convictions, which they had a right to hold, the methods of all the factions left much to be desired. They tried to use a concerted effort to influence the church direction. After a period of trying to please everybody the pastor eventually had to resign his post at the church. In this case the concerted pressure and expectations of the anti-spiritual-gifts lobby eventually won through. The expectations of others can thus frustrate the manipulated person, leaving him or her unable to do what they think is right, while weighing them down with the expectations of others.

3. *Egocentric*

Some manipulators can be highly ambitious. The egocentric dominator will have a strong desire to be the leader of the group. He or she may sometimes appear to be encouraging others to become leaders in the group, but the extent of their authority will be minimal.

Such was the case with a pastor from a church in Middlesex. Although he had elders and deacons, they could not make one decision without his approval. It is understandable that a pastor or leader would want to have a say in any major decisions affecting the foundations or fabric of church life. In the case of this pastor, virtually every decision made in the church had to have his stamp of approval, to the extent that the deacons could not even decide on the colour of the new carpet in the ladies' toilets without his authority! Such is the hallmark of egocentric manipulators. Although they sometimes take up suggestions made by other people, they will more readily accept good ideas if they themselves appear to be the originator of these suggestions. In the group, dominators usually consider themselves superior. When they feel their position being threatened by anyone, they tend to withdraw from that person. The egocentric is a selfish individual.

Why dominators dominate and manipulators manipulate

The question many on the receiving end of manipulation or domination ask is, 'Why me?' What lies at the root of an individual's compulsion to impose his or her own will upon another? Why should it deepen into aggressive or manipulative behaviour? Why should one person seek to intimidate another into accepting a suggestion, even when they know that person would rather not take up the offer or advice?

1. *History plays a part*

There are many reasons why a person dominates others. Behaviour that has developed over a long period of time is often hardest to break. Many acquire their attitude from childhood, which makes it harder for them to accept that their learned behaviour is wrong. Included in these are people who have been so hurt in their childhood years that they diligently seek to organise everything that happens around them. These individuals are determined to make sure that they never again find themselves suffering because of someone else's bad judgement.

Others, though, may have developed a manipulative manner because the people they grew up respecting were either domineering or manipulative.

A third group may have mainly associated with individuals who refused to take responsibility. This third group has learned to take authoritative action and expects others to respond accordingly.

A fourth group has simply chosen to dominate and direct circumstances around them in a conscious, deliberate fashion. They like the feel of power and will take advantage of opportunities to wield it. These people enjoy the warped satisfaction of putting another individual into a subordinate role.

2. *Needs play a part*

Economic, social and emotional needs all play a part in the development of the hardened manipulator. I recently heard that conmen posing as beggars were intimidating people on the streets of London. Interestingly, some real beggars have adopted the same tactics. Some of these poor beggars believed that by threatening behaviour they could intimidate pedestrians into parting with money. Their economic needs caused them to abandon decent behaviour.

However, the type of dominator and manipulator I consider most disturbing is the one with emotions so darkened that he or she enjoys exercising spiritual manipulation or domination as a form of rebellion against God. A friend of mine told how his daughter's marriage turned into a nightmare. Not long after the marriage she discovered that the man she had grown to love and who was going to be the father of their child was in fact a satanist. He had come in pretending to be a Christian, but his whole intent was to cause as much hurt and damage as he possibly could. He was not only in total rebellion against God but was also pretending to be spiritual. All forms of spiritual manipulation, whether in the form of a lie in which one person tells another, 'God told me,' to blatant rebellion against God's word, can eventually lead into witchcraft: 'For rebellion is like the sin of divination, and arrogance like the evil of idolatry. Because you have rejected the word of the LORD, he has rejected you as king' (1 Samuel 15:23).

3. *Perception is important*

When Christians have assessed their circumstances without reference to the word of God, their perception, no matter how valid, cannot be approached with any measure of real faith. This is because genuine or valid faith only comes by hearing the word of God. The way an economic, social or emotional situation is perceived either causes individuals to approach it in their own strength or in the strength of the Lord. Assessing a problem without reference to the word of God as the prime source for general and specific solutions unveils a lack of trust in God. When Christians consider a situation without prior guidance from the word of God, their lack of trust in him will cause them to choose what they consider to be the best option. Usually such persons have a blind spot and do not realise that they are acting out of human ability instead of relying on God.

An individual tackling a problem or situation in his or her own strength is in danger of crossing boundaries and engaging in unrighteous activity. When a perspective devoid of the word of God is coupled with a fear of failure, the Christian is open to all sorts of temptations. To give leadership responsibilities to such Christians can be potentially limiting for a church. These individuals do not see with the eye of faith, so visions brought by others will not seem feasible or practical. Vacillating between acting and refraining from action is a common symptom of the Christian leader who acts out of uncertainty rather than from faith. This can cause many problems for a church.

Just as the Christian leader is in danger of manipulating or forcing an issue because he cannot see how it is going to work, the assessment of a dominated Christian (who perceives a limit to his or her abilities when confronted with a given situation) may be either a true or a warped one. Individuals who cannot see how to resolve their problems usually either abandon them or hand over responsibility to someone else. This sort of behaviour pattern soon becomes ingrained. A pattern of quickly dropping responsibility is often maintained even when minor decisions have to be made. Though it may appear harmless, any behaviour that evades responsibility has to be addressed. Delegation of responsibility under pressure is wrong only when it is not a shirking of duty. This pattern of dropping responsibility means that the individual soon has an unhealthy dependency on one or two other people.

Wrong dependency means pride of place goes to the dominator. Satan is seeking to entice people into worshipping him. Failing this, his desire is to manoeuvre us out of dependency upon God into dependency upon persons, objects, demons – or even formulas and methods. His aim is to destroy our relationship with God and he will use whatever means he can to do this. Jesus refused to bow down to Satan's temptations. When Satan tried to encourage Jesus into becoming dependent on what he had to offer, he met with a very stout 'Away from me' (Matthew 4:10). Only God was to be served, worshipped or depended upon.

In time we all tend to rely on who or what we feel can be trusted. If our reliance or trust is based primarily upon trustworthy people or formulas that work, then we are in danger of accepting as a priority the claims and the demands that these friends and formulas place upon our lives. How often we have said, 'Do it this way – it works,' giving praise to methods we have devised. How often we have heartily affirmed, 'There is only one thing you can do about that.' The state of our heart is revealed by whether or not there is any biblical support for such statements. To rely on any person before we rely on Jesus, or to depend on any formula that is not a principle in the word of God, is idolatry. Idolatry was something the people of Israel were warned against. They were not to give others the praise and worship due to God. Such attitudes rouse God to action: he refuses to allow worship due to him to be offered to pieces of wood, people or formulas: 'I am the LORD; that is my name! I will not give my glory to another or my praise to idols' (Isaiah 42:8).

After a public address, Herod received praise from the people of Tyre and Sidon. A lot of those who gathered to hear his speech were dependent on him for their food supply. Their dependency would account for some of their enthusiasm at what he had to say. But we must also recognise that he was an eloquent speaker (Acts 12:22). Unwisely, Herod did not turn round and redirect praise to God for his gift of eloquence, and therefore an angel of the Lord 'immediately' struck him dead.

In contrast we read that when Paul was in Lystra, he saw a man crippled from birth. Calling out to him, he told him to stand on his feet. Paul had recognised that this man was responding to the preached word. Consequently the man was instantly healed, which caused the people to respond by praising Paul and Barnabas in the Lycaonian language (Acts 14:11). Unlike Herod, Paul's response was swift when he realised that praise was being directed to them rather than to God – the apostles tore their clothes, ran into the crowd and made it clear that they were just men (Acts 14:14).

We need to consider if we praise other things before we give praise to God. Although it is right to give thanks to people and to encourage them to be helpful, we need to be aware of exactly where our dependency lies – we need to be wise.

Dominators will be opposed by God

God undertakes on behalf of godly persons: he does not leave them to the desires of the godless. Those who oppose the people of God are in a battle they will ultimately lose. In the course of his work, Paul experienced as much opposition as he had open doors to minister the gospel. While he knew what it was like to contend with the ungodly (1 Corinthians 16:9), he also experienced deliverance from their hands. The Good Shepherd will never leave his sheep unattended, but will protect and care for them.

2

Government in the Church

The most distressing place of all to find domination or manipulation is in the church. I want to stress at the outset of this chapter that I consider scriptural submission to leaders and commitment to the workings of God in a church context as highly desirable: 'Yield to your leaders and be persuaded by them. They keep watch over you as men who must give an account . . .' (Hebrews 13:17, author's own paraphrase).

Any commitment to leadership that results from a conviction by the Holy Spirit, freedom of choice and the wish to help and motivate in the church is to be commended. Commitment obtained in any other way is dubious. Unscriptural submission to leaders is a very important issue, not only to individuals who are affected but also to the whole church community. Similarly any manipulation of the church leadership by members is to be challenged.

The fruits of manipulation in the church

In the early church, unity was considered to be an important aspect in the life of the church (1 Corinthians 1:10–13). What the Spirit required was a deep unity of mind and heart among Spirit-guided believers. However, at Corinth factionalism had occurred and so Paul asked believers to consider whether the Lord could really be party to their introverted factionalism. Unity of thought and heart was being jeopardised by their worldly conduct, which among other things included the idolisation of men.

There is a fine line between honouring a person of God and idolising them. However, this line must never be crossed, because once a party spirit has found a foothold it is difficult to uproot. Paul, writing to the church at Corinth about AD 50, a year after his first letter, mentions his fear of finding factions in the church (2 Corinthians 12:20). Forty-six years later Clement, a leader in the church at Rome, still had to write to the Corinthian church reprimanding some young men who had formed a breakaway group. This indicates how deeply factionalism can set in if allowed. Jesus' example was clear: God is to be the focal point of the expression of our lives. Jesus would not let even his own family divert his attention from the centrality of God's will for his life (Matthew 12:48–50).

Factionalism has four stages. First, there must be a divergence of opinion. When this is not handled properly it produces a lot of tension and some quarrelling. The resultant strong emotions set the backdrop and foundation for factionalism. Secondly, a lining up occurs behind certain leaders or with a certain group that holds the same view.

Though these different groups can sometimes come together when they face a common enemy the differences usually come to the fore once the enemy has been disposed of. Thirdly, having drawn the battle lines, slander becomes the most effective tool available to cut down all opposition, though I have sometimes heard of violence being used in extreme cases. Fourthly, contempt for all other factions develops, and coming together as an effective body becomes more difficult as broken relationships grow.

Such behaviour hinders the church from experiencing the kind of miracles that accompanied the early disciples. To participate in a similar realm to the early disciples, in which they enjoyed tremendous responses to the preaching of the gospel and saw amazing miracles, we must have devoted leadership and co-operative members.

> They devoted themselves to the apostles' teaching and to the fellowship, to the breaking of bread and to prayer. Everyone was filled with awe, and many wonders and miraculous signs were done by the apostles. All the believers were together and had everything in common. Selling their possessions and goods, they gave to anyone as he had need. (Acts 2:42–5)

More often than not, leaders have been chosen using worldly standards rather than devotion to God. Questions such as 'What has he or she achieved in life?' have outweighed more important spiritual considerations in the selection of suitable candidates for leadership. The worldly approach has spread to all aspects of church life and so the world, which once looked to the church for leadership and direction on moral and social issues, finds it impossible to take the church seriously. When people turn to the church for help what they often see is a pale reflection of themselves. They see acceptance of homosexuality in some quarters and excuses made for a whole variety of sins. As a direct consequence the world has little respect for the church's moral stance.

Methods of manipulation in the church

Manipulation in the church can emanate from the leaders, be directed at the leaders or be imposed by one member against another. The individual spirituality of a leader will determine how successful any attempt to dominate is. Elders who are not active in their prayer life are bound to be the most open to manipulation, for it is in prayer that fellowship with the Lord is maintained. In this place of prayer leaders receive direction from God. If direction is not coming from God, then, at best, it will be coming from the personal aspirations of the leaders. Where these leaders are spiritually weak they will lean on others in the church who appear spiritually strong.

1. *Influence*

Hierarchical church structures are often used by the influential manipulator as a lever for achieving personal desires. Different reasons will account for these members being regarded as prominent. Some, for instance, have clout because of their social status or financial standing. In a certain church I visited in Scotland the elders had a vision, but then began to vacillate. This proved quite frustrating for the fellowship. When I asked why, one of the elders replied,

'We recognise God is moving us on, but some influential members don't accept that what we are doing is right. Therefore the elders feel we should stay where we are.'

When I saw them three years later they were still waiting. The influential members the elder was talking about were actually the wealthy members of the church. What had alarmed the elders was the attitude of some rich members at the church business meeting. They had been unashamedly vocal about what they would do with their money if the leaders of the church continued to pursue the course they had embarked upon. Some of these wealthy members immediately stopped giving their tithes and as a consequence the church was beginning to struggle financially. It was at this point that the leadership gave in to the pressure. Financial manipulation often results in church plans becoming tailor-made to fit the opinion of the 'influential' few. Having once bowed down to financial manipulation the leadership soon develop a learned response pattern. Such manipulators know that by bringing a little pressure to bear the leadership will bow to the manipulators' will. The best thing an individual church member can do is to confront the leaders and ask them if they feel intimidated by any form of financial manipulation. If they do, then through the ordinary members' prayer support the leaders can stand up for the plans they know God has given the church.

Many ministers are finding their hands tied by financial manipulators in the church. We should provide prayer and any other support we can give the church leadership, to ensure that they maintain integrity in their decision making. If you are in a position of leadership, become resolved in your faith. Believe that where you seek first God's kingdom and his righteousness all things will be given to you (Matthew 6:33). This includes finance for the church.

2. *Evasion of responsibility*

Some leaders evade responsibility as a means of keeping a particular equilibrium in the church. When pressed to use their rightful authority they refrain. The weak and insecure leader realises that playing one stream of thought against another while never quite revealing his own opinion can be a powerful way of keeping the status quo in the church. Unfortunately factionalism can develop where there is no strong leadership team, resulting in members who are not in leadership attempting to provide direction in the church.

I remember visiting a certain pastor called Sam. We sat down for tea, chatting informally about the church he pastored, and he told me about how he felt the church was progressing in God. During our discussions I asked him about the praise and worship in the church, 'Is it not time perhaps to have a few more praise and worship songs?' At this point Kay his wife interjected, 'That would be a good idea, especially as old hymns once an aid in worship are now being sung parrot fashion.' 'Yes,' said Sam, 'but we must consider the other members. Don't you realise that we need to keep pace with them all?' I explained that he needed to keep pace with the work of the Holy Spirit rather than members of his church. After encouraging him to reconsider, I pointed out that he needed to make it absolutely clear where the leadership team believed God was leading the whole church in the realm of praise and worship. He began to use emotional manipulation, evading responsibility by hiding behind others in his church. He emphasised that he thought it best to leave the matter of praise and worship to Gordon the worship leader.

I asked Sam if he agreed that praise and worship in any church is a collective leadership responsibility. All the leaders surely have the responsibility to ensure that the church is generally going where God wants it to, especially in praise and worship, and not where the music director alone thinks best. But Sam still refused to accept overall responsibility – although he recognised the problem, he shirked the obligation of leadership.

The tension many church leaders feel between keeping the reins on the fast-moving members of the church, and going at the pace of the slowest member, is a difficult one. Such a strain only ever leaves the door open for manipulation where it is allowed to enter the realm of church politics. If a leader keeps a clear vision before the church, much of the tension in the membership will disappear. The stronger the vision and direction, the less likely leaders will be to evade responsibility for direction and duty.

Leaders who, in seeking to keep the peace, resort to preaching a gospel of compromise, will never see the signs and wonders that Jesus promised would accompany the preaching of his gospel. This is because they are preaching compromise, not the gospel. I felt really sorry for Sam. Though he was sitting on the fence, he could see the wonder-ful things that God was doing around the country and wanted to be a part of it. Sam's problem is one that many leaders face. A longing to move with God, but not enough courage to break the mould of traditions and fears. Sam real-ised that there would be a cost involved in moving with God. Over the years he had become battle weary and felt that he had gone through his fair share of personal attacks. Knowing that some would leave and others would be upset, he was not prepared to pay the cost necessary to move in the vision of God.

3. *Dogmatism*

Scripture clearly commands that we should hold firmly to right doctrine. Salvation itself depends on what we believe about Jesus. Therefore the study of the Scriptures is important, as it is one of the ways in which we show ourselves approved of God: 'Watch your life and doctrine closely. Persevere in them, because if you do, you will save both yourself and your hearers' (1 Timothy 4:16).

Unfortunately some Christians take this and other scriptures as a licence for asserting their strong views on points of Scripture. An inflexibility of attitude and intensity in communicating doctrine is fairly characteristic of the dogmatic. Missing in their exposition is patience, love and humility. Though we need to hold right doctrine, the presentation of that doctrine is important. The way it is delivered must be in keeping with the doctrine being delivered.

Dogmatism is an inflexibility that refuses to see any other point of view. What is alarming is the speed at which such inflexibility can quickly introduce factions into a small fellowship. The best way for leadership to combat this is to explain how important it is to be open to the possibility of being wrong over any interpretation of Scripture.

4. *Gnosticism*

'Spiritual Gnostics' (my term) are just as bad as the dogmatic. These are characterised by their mystical approach to circumstances. I borrow the term 'Gnostic' from a sect that plagued the church in the first two centuries after the resurrection of Jesus. The only similarity, though, is in the way that spiritual Gnostics claim to possess information or knowledge that often goes against biblical authority. They act as if they know every secret contained in heaven itself. Their behaviour generally results in abuses of the gifts of the Spirit.

In the summer of 1990 I was leading a series of early morning prayer meetings at a Christian camp. The prayer meetings were attended by over three hundred people. During one of the meetings a prophecy was spoken in which God asked us to be quiet before him. In this time of quietness some people knelt before the Lord, while others lay prostrate, and the power of God was present. A couple of people began to experience deliverance while others simply melted before God and wept silently. Suddenly during this precious time a certain lady decided to give a long oration about the progress of the camps. After a while I gently but urgently cut in and corrected her by saying God had asked us to be quiet.

While we waited upon the Lord, people continued to burst into tears as God moved among us in the silence. Yet again, just before I was about to close the prayer meeting, that same lady came up to me and said that she believed God wanted her to finish what she had been saying. She was a spiritual Gnostic. What struck me about her was that she was sincere, genuinely believing that she was right in sharing what she had to share. I thought that this was commendable, but what revealed the true state of her heart was the way in which she had responded to correction. The need to speak out what she considered to be right was more important than how I felt God was leading the meeting. Typical of the spiritual Gnostic, she could not submit to authorised leadership.

I have often seen pastors surrounded by such people. Just before the pastor gets up to preach, a handful of notes considered to be 'words' from God for the church are thrust into his hands. While some undoubtedly are from the Lord to encourage the church, others unfortunately come from the spiritual Gnostics. The things they believe to have been revealed to them have to be shared with the whole congregation. Woe betide the pastor who does not find room to share their particular 'word'.

Dealing with charismatic Gnostics can be quite difficult in a church context. They are often frustrated people who pass on this frustration and spiritual Gnosticism to others who come under their influence in the church. To offend the Gnostic is to invite the wrath of the Gnostic clan. I have noticed that some pastors normally try to appease them by sharing what they have to say, albeit in some watered-down form.

During my travels I have come across some overwhelming spiritual Gnostics, and find them extremely difficult to work with. Where there is weak leadership the charismatic Gnostic could, with enough pressure, be the one responsible for the direction of the church. Potentially they are much more dangerous than the financial blackmailer, not only because pronouncements are made that affect doctrine, but because such assertions are made in the name of God. They will tend to gather around that leader who is the weakest and use him as a platform for expressing their own beliefs.

5. *Wrong prayers*

The whole of the Bible has to be understood through the life and work of Jesus Christ. Jesus told us to love our enemies, not pray against them. God would rather we pray for those who oppose the message of the gospel.

When Jesus was not well received in a certain Samaritan village the disciples wanted to offer up unchristian prayers:

> And he sent messengers on ahead, who went into a Samaritan village to get things ready for him; but the people there did not welcome him, because he was heading for Jerusalem. When the disciples James and John saw this, they asked, 'Lord, do you want us to call fire down from heaven to destroy them?' But Jesus turned and rebuked them. . . . (Luke 9:52–5)

I have sometimes heard Christians offer up such prayers. Instead of asking God to see and deal with rebellion against the gospel, they resort to the kind of raw prayers Jesus told his disciples to refrain from. Later in Acts 4:23–31 we see a much more mature Peter and John just out of prison. When they raise their voices with the other disciples it is not to ask God to rain down fire or any other such calamity upon the chief priests and rulers of Israel who are opposing them. No, their request is that God should take note of the threats of the rulers, and then stretch forth his hand to heal and perform signs and wonders. Instead of curses upon the opposition they ask the blessing of God as they preach the word.

Praying people out of positions of leadership, or asking God to remove people from leadership, comes very close to

calling fire down from heaven. Scripture makes it clear that
God himself places people in positions of authority:

> Everyone must submit himself to the governing authorities, for
> there is no authority except that which God has established. The
> authorities that exist have been established by God. (Romans
> 13:1)

Authority can only ever be flouted where it is either bibli-
cally considered to be immoral or where it departs from the
lifestyle Jesus expects a child of God to live. The kind of
prayers that we should offer up for those who oppose the
gospel should centre on the blessing of God. When people
use prayers as a vehicle to pull people down it has more in
common with witchcraft than the kind of love and goodwill
that should be fundamental to our prayers. God is not in the
business of 'zapping' people we disagree with, simply
because they have got it wrong. Asking him to do this is the
wrong approach in prayer: 'I urge, then, first of all, that
requests, prayers, intercession and thanksgiving be made for
everyone' (1 Timothy 2:1). In our prayers should be the
flavour of thanksgiving for the individuals we are praying
for. If a person cannot honestly give thanks for an individual
or ask God to bless them before, during and after prayer,
then he or she should not bother. Manipulative prayers do
little more than colour the opinion of others about the people
featured in those prayers.

Another form of abuse of prayer is the individual who
uses prayer as a vehicle for manipulation in the prayer
meeting. This individual waits to hear what everyone else
prays and then follows those prayers by praying in a way

that corrects the previous prayers he or she considers offensive. Everyone usually just ignores it. When such prayers are spotted, the leaders need to address the wrong attitude behind them. Real love and care for the fellowship means rejection of all forms of wrong attitude: wrong prayers thus should not be ignored.

Addressing the problem in the church

Any person of God has to come to a point where he or she finally realises that unless they attempt to take hold of a vision from God, they will be buffeted by the whims of everyone else. The apostle Paul took measures to maintain unity, but in doing this he did not allow himself to be compromised by dogmatic brothers from Jerusalem. These sought to add rules and amendments to the gospel Paul preached to the Gentiles (Galatians 2:2–5). He faced an intensity of opposition few of us have ever come across. The traditionalists from Jerusalem wanted to bind and frustrate the message, believing there were certain traditions the Gentile converts had to accept. Paul could have been swayed or have settled for an easy life – instead he held on to his revelation from God and explained it to the leaders at Jerusalem.

In speaking to the other recognised leaders at Jerusalem he avoided a possible major split between the Jews and the Gentiles in the early church. The apostle Paul refused to sit on the fence. Peter, however, came under the pressure of the same Jewish traditionalists, and it caused him to behave hypocritically. Rather than allow such behaviour to go unnoticed Paul challenged Peter:

When Peter came to Antioch, I opposed him to his face, because he was clearly in the wrong. Before certain men came from James, he used to eat with the Gentiles. But when they arrived, he began to draw back and separate himself from the Gentiles because he was afraid of those who belonged to the circumcision group. The other Jews joined him in his hypocrisy, so that by their hypocrisy even Barnabas was led astray. When I saw that they were not acting in line with the truth of the gospel, I said to Peter in front of them all, 'You are a Jew, yet you live like a Gentile and not like a Jew. How is it, then, that you force Gentiles to follow Jewish customs?' (Galatians 2:11–14)

Even the first apostles had to make sure that they did not succumb to the pressure of religion. Religious people can be either docile or dominant. The main problem in the church context is a great unwillingness to change: it may not always be hotly resisted but will usually have no participators from the religious ranks. Thus new forms of praise and worship, methods of outreach or orders of service are subjects of complaint. One way to spot a religious person is through the trappings that go with their religion: for example, lots of symbols such as crosses and other religious articles may adorn such a person's house. Though such people can be serious about God they can appear to be more interested in the trappings of their religion than with him.

Heavy shepherding

At the beginning of this chapter I stressed the need for right governmental authority in the church. When this goes wrong serious long-term problems arise. 'Heavy shepherding' or heavy discipleship seeks to tie people into a relationship in which one believer obeys another without question. This usually takes the form of a pyramid structure in which group leaders are submitted to a church leader who is submitted to an area leader who has many pastors under him.

God does not want pastors or leaders to dominate and control every aspect of the lives of church members. Heavy shepherding is wrong because it takes away the individual's freedom to choose. People should not be treated like children who can't manage their own affairs. God does not want the shepherds to lord it over the sheep: he himself served the whole of humankind when he came to earth to work out the plan of redemption. Shepherds in the kingdom are meant to be servants.

Where heavy shepherding or heavy discipleship has influenced a church, those affected by it will invariably find it difficult to make decisions for themselves. This is because they will have learned to listen and accept the word of their 'shepherd' without question. Because the leaders in the movement have asked people to follow them, they have unwittingly placed themselves as intermediaries between the individual and Jesus.

The call in the word of God is to follow Jesus, not leaders. If we follow leaders we will eventually behave like the leaders we are following, rather than like Jesus. *We don't follow men of the word, rather we follow 'the Man' who is 'the Word'*. Paul told the Corinthians to take heed of the life he lived:

Therefore I urge you to imitate me. For this reason I am sending to you Timothy, my son whom I love, who is faithful in the Lord. He will remind you of my way of life in Christ Jesus, which agrees with what I teach everywhere in every church. (1 Corinthians 4:16–17)

Paul asked the Corinthian Christians to imitate him, but he took care not to ask them to follow him. His desire was that the Corinthians would imitate him in the way he lived for Christ and his obedience to the word of God. So, we can see that there is a world of difference between some leaders who have asked people to follow them and Paul who did not.

Some of the heavy shepherding practices of recent decades may have sounded good but the results were ultimately damaging. Some leaders felt the need 'to make disciples' as Jesus instructs believers (Matthew 28:19), but though it is our responsibility to make disciples it is not right to force discipleship on anyone. Discipleship is a response to a divine call, a desire to submit to godly instruction. For discipleship to be successful there must be flexibility and room for the Holy Spirit to move and work in each individual's life. Most of the discipleship or heavy shepherding movements have taught principles by which to live. Though principles in the word of God help, the problem is that unless the Holy Spirit has been allowed to convict, individuals learn to live by rigid rules handed down to them rather than in relationship with God. They learn to relate to and obey their 'shepherd' rather than 'the Shepherd'.

It is a fallacy to think that Christians desperately need strict discipleship to grow. Paul only visited Thessalonica for about two-and-a-half to three weeks and was then run out of town (Acts 17:1–14). But later he was still able to write to a thriving church, 'How can we thank God enough for you in return for all the joy we have in the presence of our God because of you?' (1 Thessalonians 3:9).

The church in Thessalonica had survived although it had

not received the kind of grounding that Paul had hoped to give it. Undoubtedly it was the word of God that brought about the fruitfulness in the lives of the Thessalonians. It is also not the personality, as already mentioned, that conveys the word of God, but the word of God itself that brings about fruitfulness in an individual's life. The person who speaks forth the word of God helps only because of the results the word of God has produced in his own life. Leaders are to guide by example, not govern by decree.

For right discipleship to be in operation the following points will be helpful:

1. If an individual is under your care, don't use your position to force them to do anything against their will.
2. Don't run down individuals looking for help and guidance, but help them to understand how they are getting things wrong.
3. Allow the Holy Spirit to do the convicting.
4. Remember they are not your disciples – they belong to Jesus.
5. Don't smother the convert in a tight relationship. Allow them to move on or away if they want to.

Discipleship is a command of the Lord, and where it is rightly applied it does wonders for the spiritual development of an individual.

3

Friends and Family

It is important to stress that in this chapter we will not be focusing on the things that produce a good relationship; rather, we will look at the things that can adversely affect our relationships. We will seek to understand what kinds of roots could lie at the bottom of unhealthy and wrong relationships so that we can pull them out and plant in their place the healthy seed of the word of God.

Friends

Friends influence some of the most important decisions of our lives. Undoubtedly we all like having friends. Given the great need we all have to be acquainted with a good friend we can see how easily relationships can be abused. Alternative motives occasionally take over and cause individuals to act in manipulative ways.

Sexual manipulation

Some have said that sexual magnetism cannot be helped: 'You either have it or you don't.' The fact is, as long as you are a human being you have it. God made men and women to be sexual creatures. Of course sex is meant to be expressed purely within the bounds of marriage (Acts 15:29; Leviticus 20:10).

It may be surprising, but it is true that some friends will either consciously or subconsciously attempt to influence by using sexual chemistry. Both men and women can be guilty of this. Sexual chemistry is powerful; it can motivate people into doing extraordinary things – even murder. When David caught a glimpse of Bathsheba he ended up murdering her husband. His temptation came through what he saw:

> One evening David got up from his bed and walked around on the roof of the palace. From the roof he saw a woman bathing. The woman was very beautiful, and David sent someone to find out about her. The man said, 'Isn't this Bathsheba, the daughter of Eliam and the wife of Uriah the Hittite?' (2 Samuel 11:2–3)

What is taken in by the eye often influences the heart, and can easily capture the soul. The person who flirts is an example of the sexually manipulative. Enticed persons find themselves being teased with the possibility of a romantic encounter. If the person being tempted is not mindful of the things of the Holy Spirit, the first thing that happens is that they enter a short period of confusion from which they either succumb to the manipulator or emerge victorious in Christ. Single people have to be especially careful. It only takes one desperate individual to manipulate sexually, but the victim, whether single or married, may be left with the consequences for the rest of his or her life.

People who are exasperated by others who constantly pick up the wrong signals sometimes say in counselling situations, 'I can't seem to help it; people always seem to get the wrong signal no matter what I do.' Though I do accept that some men and women find that people sometimes misconstrue, I also believe that all men and women have it within their power not to send wrong sexual signals to the opposite sex. For instance, a lady who finds that men seem to be overly attracted to her might find it wise to dress more modestly. This may seem like a drab and boring way to live, but which is more important, the problem that could eventually lead both you, and perhaps a friend, into sin, or a solution that protects both you and your friends?

A man may also find that because he is handsome a lot of girls flock around him. I would encourage such people to do their best to ask their male friends for help or favours as a priority over asking doting fans! These girls are not only vulnerable because they are 'smitten', but they are also open to manipulation because they want to win the man's heart.

All flirting is wrong and cannot be justified. It leads into wrong sexual fantasies and may eventually lead to adultery or fornication. Demons can also use the sin of sexual manipulation to gain a foothold in an individual's life, and sexual manipulation does not only happen with single people. I have counselled people who have told me that the other partner makes many demands on them and even uses the threat of 'no sex' as a weapon to get their own way. Husbands and wives have to agree that arguments and disagreements must not find their way into the marriage bed. In other words, all problems should be sorted out before bedtime, never during lovemaking (Ephesians 4:26).

Premarital dangers

In an attempt to understand some of the sources or causes of manipulation sometimes taken into a marriage, we will look at some premarital attitudes.

1. *The question of compatibility*

One of the main goals or desires of the majority of people is to find a partner with whom they can share the joys and fruits of intimate and personal relationship. When things far removed from the idyllic premarital dream take shape in the marriage, then marriage itself can become a source of frustration and resentment. Before long the couple may be locked into what seems a never-ending battle. When blockages are present in a marriage one partner may decide to help the other see the error of his or her ways. The spirit in which this is done will either help or hinder. Praise God that most marriages have vast areas of compatibility and, where there is willingness, time and mutual prayer, a couple can usually move away from the extremes that heighten the tension. But when blockages do arise due to differences in temperament and attitude they can cause the sturdiest of marriages to take a buffeting.

The marital vows are a lifelong commitment. So what happens if one partner is much more spiritually inclined than the other? Or if one enjoys loud praise and worship and the other does not? Such differences in taste or spiritual growth can cause serious emotional turbulence.

What then is the difference between the spouse who 'complements' and the one who is 'compatible'? Compatible spouses who are generally congenial resolve difficulties by assenting to the other partner's positive points. The compatible find a level where they flow in harmony. On the other hand spouses who complement each other supplement each other's activities. They behave like extensions of the other person, representing an expansion or continuation of the other partner. These are companions: like associates they are dedicated to the same goals. When interacting with one of these partners it is like working with a likeness of the other. If we distinguish between the compatible spouse and the one who complements, it will help us understand exactly what couples mean when one of them says, 'He is not what I expected,' or 'She doesn't seem to care about the things I care about.'

To achieve a good marriage generally requires a mix of both of these distinctions specific to each couple. Some people only realise after selecting a mate that it is impossible to demand, produce or impose the specific mix we want without damaging the other person's self-esteem or sense of worth. The production of the right mix between compatibility and complementing is only properly achieved with God's help and with consideration for the other partner.

2. *Secret personal expectations before marriage*

Before marriage most couples like to think they have the most open relationship in the world. But the truth is, most couples do not fully express or communicate their priorities in life, and usually fail to explain what they are expecting from the marriage. The underlying assumption is that the partner should automatically know these things. Then when within the commitment of marriage one partner suddenly finds that the other seems to be overlooking some of these undisclosed expectations it can lead to great mental stress and a withdrawing of intimacy. When the other spouse notices a withdrawal of intimacy by his or her partner, he or she does not understand the rejection. In an attempt to break through the cold response to advances the rejected partner will usually play up to the withdrawing partner, even giving in to requests not normally acceptable. Withdrawing in this way is sometimes used as a means of manipulating a partner.

3. Expectation of in-laws

When a man and woman marry they become one flesh with the view of building their own home and family. The old emotional and financial attachment to parents should completely change: 'For this reason a man will leave his father and mother and be united to his wife, and they will become one flesh' (Genesis 2:24). Marriage is not an evolution in relationships but a maturing of the old relationships. The in-laws have to respect the new unit's individuality and personal responsibility.

In-laws who cannot fully let go of a child cause unnecessary problems. The stress of losing your daughter or son to another person can be an experience difficult to bear or contemplate. An upset in-law may be seeking to intervene for a whole plethora of reasons. He or she may have just lost a life-long partner and perhaps finds the thought of losing a loving son or daughter and then being left alone much too hard to bear. Instead of trying to work out an acceptable solution, such an in-law may act up, making unrealistic demands. Parents may be emotionally dependent upon a child for a variety of reasons, including being starved of emotional input from a partner, or because they were not really loved by their own parents when they were children. The child who is leaned upon because of such traumatic or hurtful incidents may find that his or her parent continues to make emotional demands after marriage. Children responding to parental emotions as a priority over the spouse's emotional needs can place considerable strains upon a marriage. In-law pressure can be avoided, however, by the couple talking through and verbally affirming the priority of their own emotional needs over the needs of in-laws. This will remove a lot of tension and help to win co-operation between a couple and their in-laws.

4. *Right roles within the family*

The importance of right roles within a family first struck me at a conference in High Leigh. The speaker emphasised the differences in roles between a man and a woman. It was then that I became aware that the disintegration of female and male roles was indeed a major problem that not only affects the world but also the church.

To ensure that husbands and wives relate to one another in a godly manner, and to ensure that children are treated with respect and dignity in the home, it is important to have a clear understanding of the roles God has outlined for right family relationships. These guidelines for living have been clearly established in the Scriptures.

Nowadays many men find it difficult to affirm that they are the head of the home. Often when a man does have the courage to do this he hastily qualifies it with statements such as 'but I believe that my wife is an equal partner in the marriage' or 'but my wife has an equal say in what happens'. Such statements reveal an insecurity or fear that they will be labelled as domineering or chauvinistic. While there is still a need to affirm the place, value, dignity and equality of women, and while women have suffered much injustice under the hand of men, it is important that affirmation of women is not done in a way that devalues the role of men. I believe it is abundantly clear in Scripture that men and women are equal in God's eyes.

The role a husband is required to play, regardless of equality, is that of head of the home. He is the authority figure in the house. But his authority must be the authority of one who is first submitting his life and plans to God. 'Husbands, love your wives, just as Christ loved the church and gave himself up for her' (Ephesians 5:25). Husbands are not meant to lord it over their wives but should show respect for their partners. This is a vital aspect of godly living and will help secure an effective and unhindered prayer life:

> Husbands, in the same way be considerate as you live with your wives, and treat them with respect as the weaker partner and as heirs with you of the gracious gift of life, so that nothing will hinder your prayers. (1 Peter 3:7)

The role that wives are to play is that of helpmeet to the husband, a priceless support. Nevertheless wives are expected to submit to their husbands:

> Wives, submit to your husbands as to the Lord. For the husband
> is the head of the wife as Christ is the head of the church, his
> body, of which he is the Saviour. (Ephesians 5:22–3)

The behaviour of women in home and church should be one
that wins them respect (1 Timothy 3:11). To be submissive
does not mean that a wife should become subservient or
second class.

The husband has a responsibility to make the home a
secure place, providing for the family, while the wife has the
responsibility of making the home an emotionally stable
place (Proverbs 31:10–31). Home should always be a place
close to the heart. The people of Israel longed for home when
they found themselves captives in a foreign land: 'By the
rivers of Babylon we sat and wept when we remembered
Zion' (Psalm 137:1). The tears they shed were for a variety of
reasons, but in this psalm the people of Israel, now captives
in Babylon, were remembering the joy of being free in their
own land and country. In a similar way the home should be
thought of as a place of sanctuary and rest, not as a place of
conflict and strife or bondage.

Children and parental duties

1. *The home is a place of sowing into young hearts*

If children are to grow up living in a Christlike manner it is
necessary to teach them the right things from an early age.
The people of Israel were commanded to educate their children as they journeyed on to the Promised Land:

> These commandments that I give you today are to be upon your
> hearts. Impress them on your children. Talk about them when

you sit at home and when you walk along the road, when you
lie down and when you get up. Tie them as symbols on your
hands and bind them on your foreheads. (Deuteronomy 6:6–8)

In Deuteronomy the concept is of educating the children not
just by a single act but through a continuous education. If
you eat a lot of fatty food you grow fat; if you eat a lot of lean
meat and non-fatty food you have a good chance of remain-
ing slim. I once saw an advert that read, 'What you eat is
what you are.' It could also be said that what you take in
spiritually is what you are spiritually. The important
element in childhood is the word of God. If a child is fed on
a diet of pork pies he or she will grow up overweight, but a
child fed on a well-balanced diet will grow up healthy. In the
same way we know that children who are taught and trained
according to the word of God will probably grow up to live
out what they were taught. Even if a child backslides or
turns away from God, the good principles of the word of
God will be deeply entrenched in their personality.

The things that happen in the home will affect and govern
the formative years of a child's life. Children learn by imitat-
ing their parents. They learn by copying what they see or by
repeating what is said to them. God intended humans to
learn this way: 'Train a child in the way he should go, and
when he is old he will not turn from it' (Proverbs 22:6).

God's desire is that the first thing upon the lips of the children of his household, the church (Ephesians 2:19), should
be his word. This is the foundation that God wants to build
upon in the life of our children. It is important therefore that
the household is instructed as a unit. Consistent input as a
unit will mean a certain level of consistent growth in the life

of every member either born or adopted into the family, regardless of that member's spiritual state. This was the case with the early church: 'You know that I have not hesitated to preach anything that would be helpful to you but have taught you publicly and from house to house' (Acts 20:20).

2. A social awareness of home

A wrong understanding of what constitutes a good home can give rise to a divided house. God teaches that the home is to be a place of honour and solidarity (Exodus 20:12). Harmony in a household can be achieved when there is an understanding of individual responsibilities in the house. Unanimity can be achieved in a household when collective responsibility is highlighted and spelt out. God taught his people that the behaviour of individuals in his family affected the life of every member.

When the people of God marched against Jericho God kept his covenant and acted faithfully by helping Israel to defeat them. But Achan had been unfaithful and had taken some of the spoils back home with him, something God had commanded the people not to do. Because of Achan's disobedience, God's anger burned against all Israel. When they went up to do battle against the city of Ai, they were defeated and routed, causing Joshua to seek God. One man had committed the offence but God regarded the whole family of Israel as guilty.

> Israel has sinned; they have violated my covenant, which I commanded them to keep. They have taken some of the devoted things; they have stolen, they have lied, they have put them with their own possessions. (Joshua 7:11)

Achan was later punished for his crime (Joshua 7:16–26). But the lesson should not be lost. Though each person is now responsible for his or her own sin (Ezekiel 18), the behaviour of any member of the family will have a bearing on the rest.

Individual responsibility must be explained to members of the household by the parents, for a good home is where children grow up in an atmosphere where the roles of each family member are spelt out clearly. Likewise the church that is the household of God has certain duties each member of the household is expected to perform. Here is a general list from Colossians 3:18–4:1 and Ephesians 5–6 outlining some of the duties a family member has towards the others (using the wider meaning of the word 'family' explained below):

1. Husbands, love your wives and do not be harsh with them.
2. Wives, submit to your husbands as to the Lord.
3. The wife must respect her husband.
4. Husbands, love your wives, just as Christ loved the church and gave himself up for her.
5. In this same way, a husband ought to love his wife as his own body, which he feeds and cares for.
6. Fathers, do not exasperate your children, or they will become discouraged.
7. Fathers, bring your children up in the training and instruction of the Lord.
8. Children, obey your parents in everything, for this pleases the Lord.
9. 'Honour your father and mother' – which is the first commandment with a promise – that it may go well with you and that you may enjoy long life on the earth.

10. Masters, provide your slaves (extended family or hired workers) with what is right and fair, because you know that you also have a Master in heaven.
11. Slaves, obey your earthly masters in everything; and do it not only when their eye is on you and to win their favour.
12. Whatever you do, work at it with all your heart, as working for the Lord, not for men.

Each household should of course add to this list, outlining their own requirements. For instance, one of my duties in the house is to take the bin out on a certain night. If there are any manual or heavy jobs in the house, I am responsible for them. My wife, Fiona, on the other hand has full responsibility for everything that happens in the kitchen. When we are in the kitchen preparing food, for example, she can tell me how she wants me to help. However, I am responsible for making sure that all the bills are paid. Giving such clear guidelines of responsibility ensures that we respect and submit to each other. The household will learn to respect boundaries. Even though we have such clear responsibilities and boundaries we will help each other when the going gets tough. If, due to some unforeseen disaster, I forget to take the rubbish out one night and suddenly remember the next morning just as I am dashing off to work, Fiona will take it out for me to ensure that the whole house does not suffer due to my failure.

After setting unit boundaries, social boundaries can be better analysed and understood. A household should desire to live and function as a whole, proclaiming the gospel as a unit. It should recognise that as a unit of society it should affect other units surrounding it. The humanistic, socialistic and capitalistic understandings of society are corrupt and flawed, for they do not properly include a heavenly and eternal perspective. A good Christian outlook on the family home does not limit its boundaries to father, mother and the immediate children – or even to grandparents and great-grandparents – but includes those born-again Christians who have voluntarily attached themselves to the family, not just to receive but also to serve and give. Households in the Bible included servants, slaves and friends.

An understanding of the wider context of family is an important foundation for our children. This kind of social awareness in our children is vital. If children understand from an early age that social interaction is centred around God, as they grow up they will learn to evaluate the sadness of poverty and the wickedness of oppression in humanistic society, and recognise that the world seeks salvation but ignores the Saviour.

Although children are quick to take up and believe what they are taught, they are not fools. In order to assess if there is any benefit to be derived from what they are being taught, they first of all evaluate the life of their own parents, followed by the lifestyle of others within the church. If children have parents who don't live out what they preach, these youngsters will grow up with the impression that living a hypocritical life is all right, providing they assent to what is morally right, or they will rebel against everything they have been taught.

3. *Discipline*

Discipline is an important part of a child's development. It is important to use discipline wisely because it is one of the most powerful methods of controlling behaviour. If this is abused, a child can easily learn that force is the best means to acquire or achieve what they want.

The parents themselves need to live disciplined lives, otherwise a child will resent the imposition of a double standard. For children to respect their parents they need help to understand the importance of imposed boundaries and the reasons for discipline. If a child is constantly disciplined without being told why, he or she could easily grow up with resentment, and once respect is lost between a child and an adult it can be difficult to win it back. A right use of discipline is important not only for the child's sake but also for the father. If a man would aspire to be a leader in the church he must have the respect of his children: 'He must manage his own family well and see that his children obey him with proper respect' (1 Timothy 3:4).

Take Paul's recommendation of Timothy's grandmother. The examples of faith that surrounded Timothy as a young man were good and had obviously given Timothy good role models as he grew up: 'I have been reminded of your sincere faith, which first lived in your grandmother Lois and in your mother Eunice and, I am persuaded, now lives in you also' (2 Timothy 1:5).

Without punishment for wrongdoing a child will not appreciate the importance of staying within the guidelines laid down by the word of God: 'He who spares the rod hates his son, but he who loves him is careful to discipline him' (Proverbs 13:24). Parents who really love their children do not hesitate to smack them when they have done wrong. According to the Scriptures, discipline is an important part of a child's education. If a child has not developed a sense of punishment for wrongdoing how will he or she begin to understand the prospect of eternal damnation for the non-believer or disobedient? If the law did not punish a wrongdoer for wicked and antisocial behaviour many people would be hurt, abused and even murdered.

The wise parent sees discipline as a means of shaping the character and general well-being of a child's future: 'Discipline your son, for in that there is hope; do not be a willing party to his death' (Proverbs 19:18). Refusing to discipline a child thus reflects an uncaring attitude. Discipline is required to help children mature into responsible adults, for it will help them to leave behind childish ways and childish things: 'Folly is bound up in the heart of a child, but the rod of discipline will drive it far from him' (Proverbs 22:15).

Some people are afraid that if they smack their child it will make little difference and their child might end up being deprived or repressed emotionally. Others are afraid that their child might eventually reject them and rebel against them. But the Scriptures make it clear that the child will eventually benefit from such discipline: 'Do not withhold discipline from a child; if you punish him with the rod, he will not die. Punish him with the rod and save his soul from death' (Proverbs 23:13–14).

Having established the need for a scriptural approach to discipline, it needs to be stated that wrong use of discipline can cause problems for the child. A parent should only ever physically discipline a child out of love and never out of uncontrolled anger or frustration. If physical punishment is used indiscriminately, it is unlikely to have the desired effect and it can even make a child run away from home. Children so treated will almost certainly become hardened to physical punishment and may in the future ill-treat their own children.

4. *Parental love*

A mother or father's love is another powerful tool for shaping a child. Such is the power of a mother's love that personal danger is usually not considered in an attempt to save the life of a child. Moses' mother risked her life by looking after her son although Pharaoh had commanded that all male babies be killed.

> Now a man of the house of Levi married a Levite woman, and she became pregnant and gave birth to a son. When she saw that he was a fine child, she hid him for three months. But when she could hide him no longer, she got a papyrus basket for him and coated it with tar and pitch. Then she placed the child in it and put it among the reeds along the bank of the Nile. (Exodus 2:1–3)

She hid her son for an incredible three months, and during this time she could have been caught and severely punished, but her love for her child made her bold enough to hide him for as long as she could. Parents all over the world have on countless occasions demonstrated similar examples of selfless love.

Often it is said that men cannot seem to express their love to their children. I believe that every Spirit-filled believer has the capacity to break cultural norms, and display the kind of love the world seeks but will only find in Christ. Similarly the love between believing parents and their children should be the best in the world.

Though children can be selfish they recognise and respond to love when it is expressed. Showing love to a child speaks acceptance into the life of that child. Communicating love can be a positive way of teaching a child how to behave.

4

The Root Cause of All Controlling

Sin is the root of all attempts to assert ungodly domination, selfish manipulation or unscriptural control over other people. If we are to deal with manipulation it is important to understand how sinful desires give birth to manipulators.

Before Christ, the one lasting legacy handed down to all humanity from the first human was the sinful nature. Although sin has its roots in the fall of Satan and the angels who sinned with him, Adam's offence meant that the material world was infected by this disease called sin: 'Therefore, just as sin entered the world through one man, and death through sin, and in this way death came to all men, because all sinned' (Romans 5:12).

Because Adam had been given total authority over all the earth (Genesis 1:26), the consequence of his sin meant that the whole world was affected by his disobedience. Even Adam's descendants are tainted with the sinful nature because they have inherited his fallen image: 'When Adam had lived 130 years, he had a son in his own likeness, in his own image; and he named him Seth' (Genesis 5:3).

After conquering Adam, sin carried on producing wicked results in the lives of his descendants. In Genesis chapter 4 God speaks of the struggle between sin and humans in a way that almost attributes personality to sin itself. The Lord warned Cain to beware of sin, which was seeking to make a slave of him: 'If you do what is right, will you not be accepted? But if you do not do what is right, sin is crouching at your door; it desires to have you, but you must master it' (Genesis 4:7).

Sadly Cain's jealousy later mastered him, and as a consequence he killed his brother. Cain's desire to manipulate and control his circumstances came out of a desire to be accepted by God, but by allowing himself to become jealous of his brother, his longing for acceptance turned into a sinful ambition to become the sole object of God's approval.

Another individual motivated by selfish ambition was Simon the sorcerer. The book of Acts reveals that Simon was also driven by his need for recognition. Before Philip came and preached the Good News in his city, Simon was considered an important person. And like others in the city who heard the gospel, he repented of his sins and gave his life to the Lord. Yet after his conversion his heart still hungered for power, and so he decided to try to buy it from the apostles:

> When Simon saw that the Spirit was given at the laying on of the apostles' hands, he offered them money and said, 'Give me also this ability so that everyone on whom I lay my hands may receive the Holy Spirit.' (Acts 8:18–19)

Simon was driven by his need for recognition and status. He was even prepared to bribe Peter and John in an attempt to acquire the ability to impart the Holy Spirit.

Like Cain and Simon most manipulators have become captivated by selfish and sinful desires: for some it is jealousy; for others it is curiosity, and yet others are driven to manipulation because of various other lusts. Whatever the driving emotion behind the sinful desire, the word of God warns us not to indulge in any form of iniquity. The Bible takes a strong stance against all forms of ungodliness:

> sexual immorality, impurity and debauchery; idolatry and witchcraft; hatred, discord, jealousy, fits of rage, selfish ambition, dissensions, factions and envy; drunkenness, orgies, and the like. I warn you, as I did before, that those who live like this will not inherit the kingdom of God. (Galatians 5:19–21)

Sexual immorality, idolatry and the other vices listed above produce dominators and manipulators. Such vices develop bad character and self-centred individuals. While one backslider involved in sexual sin may devise means of enticing other innocent individuals into immorality, another backslider through jealousy may slander a believer in an attempt to sow seeds of doubt about that believer's character. Remember, you reap what you sow. If we are sowing to please the Spirit we reap a harvest that leads to eternal life. When we sow to please the sinful nature we are in great danger, because sin will ensnare and entangle us with its far-reaching tentacles: 'The evil deeds of a wicked man ensnare him; the cords of his sin hold him fast' (Proverbs 5:22).

The effects of sin are seen by the wise as cords that wrap

themselves around people, holding them fast so that they cannot set themselves free from the fruit their actions have produced. Sinners are therefore like Cain under the control of wicked desires.

I recall a married man called Andy who was in a financial mess. Andy longed to become more responsible with his finances but simply could not find the strength of character to handle his money. He spent whatever he had on his desires, sometimes at the expense of his family. His wife would often stand up to him reminding him of his responsibilities, but whenever she did Andy would use emotional blackmail with an implied threat to leave if he was not allowed to do what he wanted. His wife would always give in, having her whole security threatened. Finally, recognising that he needed help, he received counselling from his pastor and advice on budgeting from some of the elders. But he carried on overspending and the rising debt began to affect him physically. Whenever he thought about it feelings of nausea would come over him.

When asked why he continued to spend beyond his means his reply was, 'I *want* to stop it but just can't seem to.' Andy's response is typical of many who 'want' to take one course of action but find themselves doing something completely different. This is because there is a world of difference between what we 'want' and what we 'desire'. In the right circumstances I may not actually do what I say I 'want' to do, because my heart may not really be in it, but given the right conditions I will most likely do what I 'desire'.

What we say we 'want' has more to do with what we think we should do; it is more a rational consideration than an emotional response, but when our emotions become involved in something we want, this becomes a desire easily translated into action.

Andy 'wanted' to pay the bills before he treated himself to unnecessary luxuries. The problem was, he never seemed to get round to doing it. I counselled him and told him he needed to repent of his bad stewardship and then to ask God to change his heart and make him more excited about paying the bills and tithing. He took the first step and managed to tithe his next pay cheque. The result was that within a week God had begun to bless him financially. Andy learned an invaluable lesson from this and has not stopped honouring God since. Because he had allowed the Lord to change his heart his whole life changed.

A heart change will always produce a change in lifestyle. This is because the heart is the wellspring of life. From the heart flow the decisions that affect our lives. A heart is the seat of affections. When a person falls in love their heart becomes passionately involved and their thoughts become caught up with the loved one. Similarly when wrong desires have won a place in our hearts they occupy our thought life and produce wrong actions: 'Above all else, guard your heart, for it is the wellspring of life' (Proverbs 4:23).

The Bible speaks of the heart as symbolically representing the centre of the whole man. Figuratively speaking the heart is the centre of a man's body, soul and spirit. It governs the expression of all man's attributes – spiritual, physical, emotional, intellectual and psychological. The Jews thought of the heart as the administrator for all these. Jesus affirmed this way of thinking: 'For out of the heart come evil thoughts, murder, adultery, sexual immorality, theft, false testimony, slander' (Matthew 15:19). Therefore if we deal with wrong and sinful desires which reside in our hearts we will not manipulate others.

God's remedy for those controlled by the sinful nature

Jesus reversed the ability of sin to rule humankind. He died upon the cross to atone for sin and its consequences. His blood obliterated the power and rights that all our previous sins held over us, and so through the death of Jesus provision for release from the power of sin was made for all humanity:

> The death he died, he died to sin once for all; but the life he lives, he lives to God. In the same way, count yourselves dead to sin but alive to God in Christ Jesus. Therefore do not let sin reign in your mortal body so that you obey its evil desires. (Romans 6:10–12)

Paul points out that all who are in Christ (born again) should now count themselves dead to sin; that is, they should see themselves dead to sin's power to control them. This is because we have become subjects of a different kingdom and slaves of a new master. In the letter to the Romans Paul looked back at the struggle he had with sin:

> But I see another law at work in the members of my body, waging war against the law of my mind and making me a prisoner of the law of sin at work within my members. What a wretched man I am! Who will rescue me from this body of death? Thanks be to God – through Jesus Christ our Lord! So then, I myself in my mind am a slave to God's law, but in the sinful nature a slave to the law of sin. (Romans 7:23–5)

Paul wanted to do what was right in the eyes of God, he recognised the law as spiritual and good, yet he could not live
a life which met the requirements of the law. Sin grappled
with his mind and took him captive just as it had taken Cain
captive. His relief only came when he found newness of life
in Christ: 'because through Christ Jesus the law of the Spirit
of life set me free from the law of sin and death' (Romans
8:2).

To be able to count ourselves dead to sin is one of the
greatest liberating thoughts available to a child of God.
Many look upon themselves as simple lowly sinners in an
attempt to keep themselves humble, but unfortunately this
kind of thinking only breeds a defeatist attitude to everything that one does. I can see that over the centuries the devil
has used this kind of thinking to undermine the church.
What God wants is a church that counts itself dead to sin. We
are to remind one another that sin has no mastery over us.

If you tell a child that she is a bad girl often enough, the
child will grow up thinking that everything she does is bad;
even when she does good things, she will not be able to
accept that fact. Later on in life if you tell the grown-up child
that her work is good she may think of you as patronising
and will find it very hard to accept compliments.

Now consider the Christian who is constantly told that he
is only a sinner saved by grace, with the emphasis on 'only
a sinner'. While I agree we all make mistakes and sin at
times, I do not believe it is scriptural to dwell in a frame of
mind that thinks of oneself as 'bound to sin'. Phrases such as
'I am bound to sin at some point' are wrong. The kind of
statement we should make is 'If I sin', with the emphasis
on if. Sin no longer has any power over us because we have

already died to ourselves and now live for Christ: 'But now that you have been set free from sin and have become slaves to God, the benefit you reap leads to holiness, and the result is eternal life' (Romans 6:22).

For the believer faced with temptation, obedience is the simple recipe required for victory over sin.

Do you need to change the company you keep?

If a person has mixed with the wrong kind of friends it is often best for that individual to refrain from associating with them for a while. This is because people tend to relate to each other in predetermined patterns – as the saying goes, 'Old habits die hard.' Even people who have had a change of heart may find the habits of their old friends overwhelming.

Where domination has been taking place in a family context it is often physically impossible to step back from the situation. Therefore where there is manipulation in the family due to wrong and wicked desires, it is imperative that an individual who has repented takes advantage of the support available from his or her local church. God in his wisdom has put us in the best family of all: his family.

Freedom from sin means a better quality of life

Peter makes it clear that our lives should be of such a quality that they will convict and attract those who belong to the world (1 Peter 4:2). Such lifestyles are possible for even the weakest of Christians because we are in the kingdom of light – unlike the unbeliever who lives in the dominion of darkness. All a Christian has to do is resolve to stand for the light.

For those who 'walk in the light' (1 John 1:7) the benefits of the new life are remarkable. The faithfulness of God promotes a feeling of joy that is indescribable. If we know that we are not living in the benefits of the new life, we need to make sure that it is not because of sin. Sin robs the individual of a high quality of life: 'From the sole of your foot to the top of your head there is no soundness – only wounds and bruises and open sores, not cleansed or bandaged or soothed with oil' (Isaiah 1:6).

When Isaiah received this word the Lord was calling the people of Judah to come back into right relationship with him. The sins of the people stopped God listening to and accepting their prayers. They brought many offerings that were meaningless and had become a burden to God because of their sins, so he commanded them to stop doing what was wrong. Obedience, which is more important to God than sacrifices, is an important key to living in his promise of a full and qualitative life (John 10:10).

5

Demons and Spirits

Because a lot of people, such as spiritualists, confuse demons and other evil phenomena with the work of ghosts, it is good to ascertain whether or not ghosts, which are usually considered to be the spirits of the departed dead, can come back to manipulate or dominate our circumstances. Then, having decided the scope of their ability, we can take a closer look at the fallen angelic world, because I aim to show that fallen angels are in fact demons.

The Old Testament speaks of the new heaven and the new earth which will replace the present ones (Isaiah 65:17). This will be a place where all the blessed dead in God will live in peace. Though much is said in the Bible about the final resting states of people after the end of history, what happens to them *before* the end of history only becomes more evident in the New Testament. As Christians we accept that believers go to the present heaven, 'paradise', where Jesus is. But the Old Testament does not give much specific information about the fate and abode of the believing dead. In Old

Testament times people who die are described as residing in a place called Sheol. This was thought of as a place in which the departed dead were beyond rescue (Psalm 89:48) and from which no one could return (Job 7:9).

In a physical sense Sheol is the grave where we bury our dead. Consequently it is said that the bodies of all people, righteous and unrighteous, are laid in the grave (Genesis 44:29). But in a spiritual sense it is the place where only the wicked go upon death (Proverbs 5:5; Psalm 9:17). Those who put their trust in God have no need to fear because God delivers the devout from Sheol (Psalm 49:15).

> I will ransom them from the power of the grave;
>   I will redeem them from death.
> Where, O death, are your plagues?
>   Where, O grave, is your destruction? (Hosea 13:14)

So, to sum up, the people of Old Testament days understood that God would not abandon the righteous to such a terrible place. Every person who died physically went into the grave, but it was believed that the spirit of the righteous went to be with the Lord (Psalm 49:14–15).

In the New Testament a clearer picture emerges. This is by no means entirely clear cut, however, but is a perspective that the Jews arrived at because of God's revelations of himself through the course of their history. They had known of Enoch walking so closely with God that he 'was no more, because God took him away' (Genesis 5:24). The story of Elijah being taken up in a whirlwind to be with the Lord would have filled many Jewish youngsters and adults with awe (2 Kings 2:11). By the time of Jesus, the righteous dead are understood by the Jewish people to be in 'Abraham's bosom'. The Talmud (a source the Jews use to understand their law) mentions paradise as being 'in Abraham's bosom', and Jesus echoes the phrase when he speaks of Lazarus (Luke 16:23). But an unrighteous dead person is spoken of as being in Hades.

Hades, often unhelpfully translated 'hell', is the same place described as Sheol in the Old Testament. It is used in the New Testament to mean the temporary residence of departed persons awaiting final judgement (Luke 16:19–31). In the New Testament it is still regarded as an unpleasant place, as shown in the story of the rich man who through his wickedness found himself in Hades:

> In Hades, where he was in torment, he looked up and saw Abraham far away, with Lazarus by his side. So he called to him, 'Father Abraham, have pity on me and send Lazarus to dip the tip of his finger in water and cool my tongue, because I am in agony in this fire.' (Luke 16:23–4)

Revelation 20:12 discloses that at the end of time the only people in Hades are those awaiting final condemnation and judgement. Like their Old Testament counterparts, Christian believers have the assurance that death for them means being with God in the same way that Abraham is with God. The blessed dead are not left in the grave (Hades/Sheol) like unbelievers, but their spirits are transported to paradise to be with Jesus, exactly like the repentant thief on the cross (Luke 23:43). This is why those who have fallen asleep in Jesus will come back with him when he returns at the resurrection: 'We believe that Jesus died and rose again and so we believe that God will bring with Jesus those who have fallen asleep in him' (1 Thessalonians 4:14).

Again it is understood that though a dead person is physically buried in the grave, their spirit is either transported to Hades, if they have been ungodly, or paradise if they have received Christ. Immediately after the judgement those in paradise will become the residents of a glorious new heaven and earth, whereas those in Hades will go to a place called 'Gehenna'. During the days of Jesus, rabbis used the word 'Gehenna' to speak of the place of final punishment. Jesus maintained this meaning in the Gospels and so Gehenna is 'hell' in the English sense of the word. At the end time just before the resurrection and judgement the devil will be thrown into Gehenna (which is the same as the Lake of Fire or hell).

Both Hades and paradise have determined boundaries that cannot be broken, so in the story of the rich man, when he asks Abraham to have pity on him, Abraham replies:

'Son, remember that in your lifetime you received your good things, while Lazarus received bad things, but now he is comforted here and you are in agony. And besides all this, between us and you a great chasm has been fixed, so that those who want to go from here to you cannot, nor can anyone cross over from there to us.'

He answered, 'Then I beg you, father, send Lazarus to my father's house, for I have five brothers. Let him warn them, so that they will not also come to this place of torment.'

Abraham replied, 'They have Moses and the Prophets; let them listen to them.'

'No, father Abraham,' he said, 'but if someone from the dead goes to them, they will repent.'

He said to him, 'If they do not listen to Moses and the Prophets, they will not be convinced even if someone rises from the dead.' (Luke 16:23–31)

The chasm between heaven and earth, though, is not permanently fixed. It has been crossed by the righteous dead, but only on the specific command of the Lord, when he raised people from the dead (John 11:43; Mark 5:39–41). But the chasm fixed between people in paradise and those in Hades is spoken of in the Bible as impossible to cross (Luke 16:26). In the above passage of Luke it would appear that the chasm between those in Hades and the earth has also been fixed. Departed spirits cannot cross either chasm or come out of their fixed states (although see below the exception of Samuel).

Despite these fixed states some people on earth try to communicate with the dead: they try to speak across the divide. A simple way of explaining the divide is by describing it in terms of two people living in two separate rooms divided by a wall 20 feet thick. If we then imagine that there are no doors or windows which could be used by a person on one side to contact the other person – or tools to break down the wall – we would be close to a fair analogy. Though it is physically impossible to leave one room for another it could be possible that one could shout and be heard by the other. Thus they cannot cross over from room to room, but it may be possible for some to hear the shouting. This analogy is simple, and it would be dangerous to read more into it other than the points I am trying to make:

- There is a divide between heaven and Hades and between Hades and earth.
- Some people on earth, despite the divide, try to confer with the dead.

The Scriptures are highly critical of any activity that embraces consulting the dead (Leviticus 19:31; 20:6, 27; 2 Kings 23:24). When the Bible speaks of people being 'called up' it does not mean that they leave the spiritual region they reside in, whether it be Hades or paradise. What it does mean is that an individual is trying to establish contact with the departed dead. When contact or calling up of the dead spirit is successful, messages are relayed. One classical and extremely unusual case in the Scriptures reveals all these points and more.

Then the woman asked, 'Whom shall I bring up for you?'

'Bring up Samuel,' he said.

When the woman saw Samuel, she cried out at the top of her voice and said to Saul, 'Why have you deceived me? You are Saul!'

The king said to her, 'Don't be afraid. What do you see?'

The woman said, 'I see a spirit coming up out of the ground.'

'What does he look like?' he asked.

'An old man wearing a robe is coming up,' she said.

Then Saul knew it was Samuel, and he bowed down and prostrated himself with his face to the ground.

Samuel said to Saul, 'Why have you disturbed me by bringing me up?'

'I am in great distress,' Saul said. 'The Philistines are fighting against me, and God has turned away from me. He no longer answers me, either by prophets or by dreams. So I have called on you to tell me what to do.' (1 Samuel 28:11–15)

Saul, having disguised himself, approached a medium and asked her for help; his desire was to consult Samuel who was dead. The woman he had sought out was known to be a well-established medium, and was familiar with the results of calling up and seeing the departed dead. Most probably, like all mediums, she had only ever contacted spirits which were in Hades (the region of the departed wicked). Not all mediums are truly aware that the spirits of the departed dead go to two separate places; they are mostly deceived into thinking that all dead people go to the same region. Suddenly as she tried to 'call up' (establish contact with) this Samuel, she realised that she was seeing something she had never seen before: she saw one of the blessed dead in God. The revelation threw her into panic, causing her to shout at the top of her voice. She knew instantly that the man who stood before her was no ordinary man but the king.

This is the only case in the Bible where a believing dead person is consulted successfully. Generally the dead will not answer mediums or respond to the living, regardless of the circumstance (Luke 16:27–31). God condemns as evil and wicked all attempts to speak to departed spirits. The onus of the sin lies with the people seeking to make contact with the dead, not with those who have already departed and are waiting in paradise or Hades for the final judgement. In fact one of the reasons why Saul is said to have died is because he consulted a medium: 'Saul died because he was unfaithful to the LORD; he did not keep the word of the LORD and even consulted a medium for guidance' (1 Chronicles 10:13).

Saul had no one but himself to blame for his actions. God had already made it clear in the Torah (Old Testament) that all forms of spiritism were an abomination in his sight:

Let no-one be found among you who sacrifices his son or daughter in the fire, who practises divination or sorcery, interprets omens, engages in witchcraft, or casts spells, or who is a medium or spiritist or who consults the dead. Anyone who does these things is detestable to the LORD, and because of these detestable practices the LORD your God will drive out those nations before you. (Deuteronomy 18:10–12)

It is obvious from Luke 16 that departed spirits cannot speak to people in the world when and as they like: someone from this side of the divide needs to attempt to speak to them. Even then, however, they are in fact likely to be speaking to demons rather than the departed dead.

From what we have seen, the spirits of dead people cannot come back from their allotted states once dead, and it is usually only those engaged in the act of calling them up who actually see them. This brings us to the conclusion that, in the light of Scripture, all unbidden supernatural phenomena, such as ghosts seen in buildings, must most probably be the result of some other activity, probably demonic, and not the actions of the departed human dead. So let us now look at the abode of fallen angels.

Christians are generally aware that demons/fallen angels do not reside in paradise, but few believers have grappled with the implications of a fall by some angels prior to the fall of man. Where do these fallen beings now reside?

You were in Eden,
   the garden of God;
every precious stone adorned you:
   ruby, topaz and emerald, chrysolite, onyx and jasper,
   sapphire, turquoise and beryl.

Your settings and mountings were made of gold;
   on the day you were created they were prepared.
You were anointed as a guardian cherub,
   for so I ordained you.
You were on the holy mount of God;
   you walked among the fiery stones.
You were blameless in your ways
   from the day you were created
   till wickedness was found in you.
Through your widespread trade
   you were filled with violence,
   and you sinned.
So I drove you in disgrace from the mount of God,
   and I expelled you, O guardian cherub,
   from among the fiery stones. (Ezekiel 28:13–16)

These verses reveal the nature of the first sin ever to enter the universe. Satan, once a guardian cherub in heaven, became proud and arrogant, and this caused him and the rebellious angels with him (2 Peter 2:4) to be thrown out of heaven. Since that initial clash Satan has set about building an alternative kingdom or dominion for himself, and just as the kingdom of God will eventually be established upon the earth, Satan seeks to strengthen his rival kingdom upon the earth. The Scriptures say that this earthly kingdom will eventually be ruled by a person called 'the beast': 'The fifth angel poured out his bowl on the throne of the beast, and his *kingdom* was plunged into *darkness*. Men gnawed their tongues in agony' (Revelation 16:10, emphasis mine).

Since the fall of these angels, there have been constant confrontations between the dominion of darkness and the kingdom God is establishing. God continues to allow some of these fallen beings to roam the earth (Job 2:2; Daniel 10:13). But in Jude's letter we learn that some of them have already been bound and are being held for the day of judgement. Why does God allow only some fallen angels to roam? This is a difficult question to answer. What seems clear, however, is that God threw disobedient spirits out of heaven just as he threw Adam and Eve out of the garden. The initial punishment for humans was banishment from the Garden of Eden into the wider earth. Similarly the initial punishment for fallen angels was a casting out of heaven: 'And the angels who did not keep their positions of authority but abandoned their own home – these he has kept in darkness, bound with everlasting chains for judgment on the great Day' (Jude 6).

When Peter writes his second letter he uses the word 'Tartarus' to explain exactly where God has sent spirits that are imprisoned because they sinned and abandoned their authority. Many versions of the Bible have wrongly translated this place called Tartarus as 'hell'. In Peter's days Tartarus was thought of by the Greeks as the place where the most wicked spiritual beings were sent. A helpful paraphrase of 2 Peter 2:4 would be as follows: God did not spare angels when they sinned, but banished them to the domain called Tartarus, a special prison built for wicked spiritual beings, placing them into shadowy dungeons where they are being kept until they are judged.

We see subsequent acts of angelic disobedience in the book of Daniel (10:13–20). Here we get a glimpse of what happens in the heavenlies. Fallen angels operate in a hierarchical order. They emerge as rulers over spiritual sectors in the heavenly realms with corresponding influence over defined geographic areas. Obviously the spiritual being that was resisting God in the book of Daniel was not yet bound or imprisoned in Tartarus. Paul intimates that Christians would come up against such beings (Ephesians 6:12).

And so from our study we see that some fallen angels are bound in chains while others are actually relatively free. In the next chapter we will look at the influence such demons can have over the Christian believer.

6

How Do Demons Influence Us?

The controversy explained

Many Christians find it difficult to believe that a Christian who has been filled with the Holy Spirit can be either possessed or influenced by a demon. Yet all Christians accept that there is a spiritual struggle taking place in the heavenly realms:

> For our struggle is not against flesh and blood, but against the rulers, against the authorities, against the powers of this dark world and against the spiritual forces of evil in the heavenly realms. (Ephesians 6:12)

In this chapter we will have to change the pace of our study on manipulation, domination and control, and perhaps stretch our thinking a little further. This is because we have to address some difficult questions. In my attempt to show that evil spirits can influence a Christian's behaviour, we will have to address several questions such as the following:

1. What is the activity of fallen angels?
2. Can a Christian have a demon?
3. How do evil spirits seek to influence?
4. What deliverance has Jesus won for believers?

There is a need to tackle this subject because many Christians are uncertain about how much power or influence wicked spirits have. Despite the powerful move of the Holy Spirit through many denominations of the church across the world, the question of how a born-again believer could be possessed is often misunderstood or evaded. In a culture that is becoming increasingly open to supernatural forces through different ideologies such as the New Age movement, alternative medicine, and eastern mysticism, it is important to have a scriptural perspective on the influence and ability of demonic or supernatural forces. Either demons cannot affect a child of God, or they can. We need to be knowledgeable about what the word of God says on the subject.

I was questioned about my stand on the issue at a large Christian camp where many people experienced powerful deliverance from demons. Having always believed that a Christian could be affected by an evil spirit, due to my African background, I had no problems affirming my beliefs. But when my fiancée (now my wife) asked me to show her where in the New Testament it said that a born-again believer could be demonised, I found that I was quite unable to give a clear-cut answer on the spot. The result was a detailed examination of the Scriptures, and the conclusion of my study is contained in this chapter. I wanted to make absolutely sure that I was not mistaken or deceived, that the race

I was running was not in vain and that the doctrine I was holding was not flawed. My subjective African experiences had to be in line with the word of God, otherwise they were of no value. The result of my study of the word has helped me to answer the following questions:

1. *What is the activity of fallen angels?*

Having established in Chapter 5 that the spirits of the dead cannot come back to earth and can only speak to the living through a medium (an act that God abhors), we can only conclude that phenomena such as ghosts have to be ruled out as the spirits of the dead. Jesus refers to demons as members of Satan's kingdom, and Satan – a fallen angel himself – is called the prince of that realm.

> And the teachers of the law who came down from Jerusalem said, 'He is possessed by Beelzebub! By the prince of demons he is driving out demons.' So Jesus called them and spoke to them in parables: 'How can Satan drive out Satan? If a kingdom is divided against itself, that kingdom cannot stand.' (Mark 3:22–4)

The word of God describes the spiritual residence of most demons as desert-like. Because demons cannot stand this arid domain in which they live they will do anything to get into a human body:

> When an evil spirit comes out of a man, it goes through arid places seeking rest and does not find it. Then it says, 'I will return to the house I left.' When it arrives, it finds the house unoccupied, swept clean and put in order. Then it goes and takes with it seven other spirits more wicked than itself, and they go in and live there. And the final condition of that man is worse than the

first. That is how it will be with this wicked generation. (Matthew 12:43–5)

Where they fail to inhabit a human body demons seek to enter the body of an animal (Mark 5:11–13). Demons are not a mass of impersonal entities – they have individual names: 'Then Jesus asked him, "What is your name?" "My name is Legion," he replied, "for we are many"' (Mark 5:9). At other times Jesus would address the demon by a synonym and not its actual name:

> When Jesus saw that a crowd was running to the scene, he rebuked the evil spirit. 'You *deaf and mute spirit*,' he said, 'I command you, come out of him and never enter him again.' (Mark 9:25, emphasis mine)

The symptoms that manifest in the individuals they manipulate or dominate are often synonyms for their names. Symptoms can thus help us to identify what kinds of spirits are at work in or through an individual. In Hosea's time God said he was going to punish the people for their rebellion (Hosea 4:6–13), at the root of which was a spirit of prostitution that led the people astray. One of this spirit's symptoms was the worshipping of idols.

Demons work on the emotions. They seek to plant or awaken wrong desires that lurk within the heart. Once enticed into giving room to wicked or evil desires, we open ourselves up to manipulation by demonic forces: 'but each one is tempted when, by his own evil desire, he is dragged away and enticed' (James 1:14).

Having succeeded in encouraging the individual to have wrong desires, demons continue to work on the individual until there is a compulsive drive to act in a certain way, usually expressing their own depraved emotions through the person. For example, they display their frustration (Mark 1:23–4). They know what it is to be afraid: when they consider God they shudder (James 2:19). In their expression of emotion through an individual, they tend to drive and entice. This was the case with a demon-possessed man who met Jesus:

> Jesus had commanded the evil spirit to come out of the man. Many times it had seized him, and though he was chained hand and foot and kept under guard, he had broken his chains *and had been driven by the demon* into solitary places. (Luke 8:29, emphasis mine)

Perhaps what some people find most astonishing is that demons can speak (Mark 1:24). Sometimes when demons speak we find that they possess a great deal of knowledge, as in the confrontation between some demons and the seven sons of Sceva. These sons of Sceva tried to cast demons out of the possessed but one day came up against a powerful demon. This demon knew who Jesus was – an interesting confession! It did not know Paul, but knew about him (Acts 19:15). But it did not 'know' the seven sons of Sceva who were not Christians, which resulted in their receiving a severe beating.

2. *Can a Christian have a demon?*

It is important to address this issue before we can study further the specific ways demons seek to manipulate, because I have found that some believers don't understand how it can be possible. Others have held the view that demons can influence a believer but have been unable to substantiate this objectively from Scripture.

The argument is often: 'No demon can exist comfortably in a person within whom the Holy Spirit resides.' This is often laid out in a very strong and emotional manner and a passage is often used to back up this claim, which wonderfully proclaims that Jesus in us is greater than the spirit of the antichrist in the world:

> Dear friends, do not believe every spirit, but test the spirits to see whether they are from God, because many false prophets have gone out into the world. This is how you can recognise the Spirit of God: Every spirit that acknowledges that Jesus Christ has come in the flesh is from God, but every spirit that does not acknowledge Jesus is not from God. This is the spirit of the antichrist, which you have heard is coming and even now is already in the world. You, dear children, are from God and have overcome them, because the one who is in you is greater than the one who is in the world. (1 John 4:1–4)

The verse is preceded by a clear warning to Christians to test the spirits which operate through prophets, indicating that there are some prophets at work who are operating through a spirit alien to the Holy Spirit.

We would certainly not be surprised to find an increase in demonic activity during the ministry of Jesus. Rather, it would be surprising if wicked spirits allied with the antichrist spirit did not attempt to obstruct the mission of the Christ. Right from the beginning of his ministry we notice Jesus already having to deal with demonic powers (Mark 1:23; 7:25). But did he intimate that such powers could be at work in or through believers? In Luke 9 we read an interesting verse that is often relegated to the footnote. It is a verse that describes Jesus' response to his disciples' desire to call down fire from heaven upon some unbelievers:

> But Jesus turned and rebuked them, and he said, 'You do not know what kind of spirit you are of, for the Son of Man did not come to destroy men's lives but to save them.' (Luke 9:55)

Undoubtedly they were being influenced by a spirit alien to the Holy Spirit. We might then ask whether the disciples were saved at this point or were still unbelievers. Obviously, they could not yet have been saved, as we understand salvation to be after the event of the cross. Nevertheless like us they had confessed Jesus as the Christ and believed that he was the Son of God (Luke 9:18–24). The fact that they continued to follow him despite his plain speaking of his forthcoming murder and resurrection to life reveals that they were determined to face danger with him and live their lives for Jesus. We ask unbelievers to make a similar confession and commitment to walk with Christ so that they may be saved:

> that if you confess with your mouth, 'Jesus is Lord,' and believe in your heart that God raised him from the dead, you will be saved. For it is with your heart that you believe and are justified, and it is with your mouth that you confess and are saved. (Romans 10:9–10)

What they had believed and confessed about Christ, and the corresponding action that went along with it, proved that they had faith in Christ: 'For it is by grace you have been *saved*, through *faith* – and this not from yourselves, it is the gift of God' (Ephesians 2:8, emphasis mine).

They thus were as saved as they possibly could be before the cross – indeed they walked with Jesus and worshipped him (Matthew 14:33), knowing full well as Jews that only God should receive worship. Yet in Luke 9:55 Jesus says that in desiring to call fire down from heaven to destroy people they had given way to a different spirit. The Greek word used here is *pneuma* (spirit); it is also the word used in Luke 13:11 to describe what had kept a woman bound in sickness for eighteen years.

Jesus is not just saying that the disciples' thinking is different; he is saying that something has affected their hearts. Where there is a desire to highlight 'thinking', quite a variety of other Greek words are used throughout the New Testament (cf. Mark 6:49, *dokeo*; Luke 1:51, *dianoia*; Luke 3:23, *nomizo*). In this passage Jesus did not turn around and simply address wrong thinking or a wrong attitude as he had on different occasions (Matthew 9:4), it was not just their wrong thinking that was being highlighted, but the 'kind of spirit' that was influencing them. Though all this was still prior to the cross – which most people see as the dividing line between believers who lived long before Jesus' death and resurrection, and those who were Christians long after these events – these were believers quite unlike any who came before or after Jesus, because they walked with him when he was here in the flesh.

How about the period after the Gospels? Is there any hint of people having another spirit like the disciples did in Luke 9? My wife rightly pointed out to me that the New Testament emphasises a standard of living free from the dominion of sin:

> But thanks be to God that, though you used to be slaves to sin,
> you wholeheartedly obeyed the form of teaching to which you
> were entrusted. You have been set free from sin and have become
> slaves to righteousness. (Romans 6:17–18)

Fiona and I soon discovered, as we studied the word of God,
that there are two sides to the coin: while we have the positive ability to live in the power of the Holy Spirit free from
demonic influence, we also have the negative ability to
submit to the power of sin. This negative ability eventually
robs us of power to resist the evil influences behind the
wrong desires. Many people, however, emphasise only the
positive side of this revelation. This is much like people who
confess that God is a God of mercy but refuse to see the other
side of the coin: that he is also a God of justice. Looking at
the evidence after the cross, what do we then find? In
addressing the Corinthians Paul, like Jesus, warns against
Christians receiving another spirit:

> For if someone comes to you and preaches a Jesus other than the
> Jesus we preached, or if you receive a different spirit from the
> one you received, or a different gospel from the one you
> accepted, you put up with it easily enough. (2 Corinthians 11:4)

Here he makes it clear that just as they received the person
of the Holy Spirit after accepting the true gospel, it was
possible for a Christian to receive a different gospel and a
different spirit to go along with it. Paul indicates later in the
same chapter that the real source behind the different gospel
and the different spirit was Satan. 'And no wonder, for
Satan himself masquerades as an angel of light. It is not surprising, then, if his servants masquerade as servants of

righteousness. Their end will be what their actions deserve' (2 Corinthians 11:14–15). Satan was the one ultimately motivating those who came to the believers with a different message.

Paul used a similar tone when he warned the Galatians not to turn to a different gospel:

> I am astonished that you are so quickly deserting the one who called you by the grace of Christ and are turning to a different gospel – which is really no gospel at all. Evidently some people are throwing you into confusion and are trying to pervert the gospel of Christ. But even if we or an angel from heaven should preach a gospel other than the one we preached to you, let him be eternally condemned! As we have already said, so now I say again: If anybody is preaching to you a gospel other than what you accepted, let him be eternally condemned! (Galatians 1:6–9)

In this letter to the Galatians, Paul warns against accepting the teaching of men or of angels who attempt to pervert the truth of the gospel.

Sin is seen in the New Testament as the means by which Satan himself can gain a foothold in the life of an individual: 'In your anger do not sin. Do not let the sun go down while you are still angry and do not give the devil a foothold' (Ephesians 4:26–7). Having learned the truth it is now up to us to live according to it, and in obedience to God.

A Christian can thus give room to a different spirit which is alien to the Holy Spirit. This alien spirit can then exercise influence over its victim. Becoming a Christian is no protection against the devil if a person then chooses to walk in disobedience to God. In the next section we will look at whether this influence is actually demon possession.

3. *How do evil spirits seek to influence?*

(a) *The battle for the mind.*   The main way demons seek to influence a person is through the mind, the major demon gateway. What a person allows to dwell in his or her thoughts will eventually dictate that person's actions, attitudes and beliefs. This is because the things an individual contemplates eventually bring him or her to a point of persuasion regarding those dominating thoughts. Prior to salvation the mind is the main area upon which Satan concentrates most of his efforts to stop a person becoming a Christian: 'The god of this age has blinded the minds of unbelievers, so that they cannot see the light of the gospel of the glory of Christ, who is the image of God' (2 Corinthians 4:4). It is by capturing a man's thoughts that Satan keeps him from turning to Christ. Any Christian will readily testify to times of great mental anxiety as they have grappled with wrong thoughts or have sought to take a stand against the devil's schemes:

> The weapons we fight with are not the weapons of the world. On the contrary, they have divine power to demolish strongholds. We demolish arguments and every pretension that sets itself up against the knowledge of God, and we take captive every thought to make it obedient to Christ. (2 Corinthians 10:4–5)

(b) *Fantasies.*   When someone tries to imagine, they are trying to form a mental picture of something. What they are trying to see may be either non-existent or not present. Imagining can have many contexts: it could be an attempt to understand what lies in store, or an attempt to place oneself in a situation that has happened. What a person is trying to imagine can be either bad or good (Ezekiel 13:17; Ephesians 3:20).

Imaginations not based upon the word of God can be a subconscious rejection of the truth, which in turn means the individual is opening up his or her mind to alternative realities. Most pop songs speak of desired but broken loves or dreams or memories. Others invite the hearer to imagine what it would be like to have a million pounds or own a private yacht, and so forth. Fantasy speaks of dissatisfaction with the life that God has given us; it only draws us into a world of unreality. These fantasies eventually lead us into sin, just like they did the people of Isaiah's day: 'All day long I have held out my hands to an obstinate people, who walk in ways not good, pursuing their own imaginations' (Isaiah 65:2).

The word of God draws out the point that people can end up pursuing what they fantasise about or allow to dwell in the imagination (Isaiah 65:2). Sexual fantasy, for example, is one of the main areas through which the enemy seeks to entrap the unsuspecting. Much of the advertising we find in our newspapers and on our television screens uses the lure of sex to encourage the individual to purchase the advertised product. This can ultimately lead to an unhealthy pre-occupation with sex and even abuse between husband and wife, where a worldly concept of sex and sexuality has been accepted as the norm.

Another means by which evil spirits may attempt to control a person's mind is through addiction. Where able, demons will cause a person to be enslaved to addictive substances – even medicines and other ordinary substances can be the means by which the human will is enticed into a state of weakness. As I once heard a friend of mine say, 'Wine is a good servant but a bad master.' Wine used medicinally can be highly advantageous, but an alcoholic suffers terribly under the influence and power of even the smallest glass of wine. Having enslaved the mind demons seek to keep an individual bound and unable to enhance his or her life.

Mental illness is one type of illness that demons try to inflict on people. This was the case with the two violently insane men in the region of the Gadarenes: 'When he arrived at the other side in the region of the Gadarenes, two *demon*-possessed men coming from the tombs met him. They were so violent that no-one could pass that way' (Matthew 8:28, emphasis mine).

Mental illness can often be due to physical injury or disability, but this is not always the cause. At a certain Christian meeting, a friend called Tim and I noticed that two counsellors were struggling with a lady who had come forward to ask for prayer. After a few minutes we asked the counsellors if they needed help.

They responded positively and introduced us to Ann who had come forward, accompanied by her friend Angela, for counselling. The counsellors told us that they had spent the last half hour trying to persuade Ann to tell them why she had come forward for prayer. When I asked Ann why she was unwilling to tell her counsellors what her need was, her response was, 'If God wants to help me then he can tell you what is wrong.' After about five minutes of trying to persuade her to tell us, Tim and I were about to give up, feeling that the most appropriate thing to do was to say a general prayer with her and then send her on her way. When I 'laid hands' upon her head to pray, the Holy Spirit immediately told me to rebuke a spirit of insanity. I responded by doing so and Ann instantly let out a terrible scream, which was the demon leaving her. The Holy Spirit further revealed that this spirit had entered Ann through her mother's side of the family. Later Angela confirmed all these 'words of knowledge' given by the Holy Spirit. The things I had prayed for were the things Ann had come to the meeting to seek help and counsel for. Ann's mother had been admitted into a mental hospital and Ann had been frightened of ending up insane herself.

Another disturbing element of satanic attack is the attempt to subject people to all forms of physical illness and sickness. People can often be bound for years by a demon and not find relief from doctors or medicines. But Jesus was able to heal all the demon-possessed who were brought to him (Matthew 8:16).

> ... and a woman was there who had been crippled by a spirit for eighteen years. She was bent over and could not straighten up at all. When Jesus saw her, he called her forward and said to her, 'Woman, you are set free from your infirmity.' Then he put his hands on her, and immediately she straightened up and praised God. Indignant because Jesus had healed on the Sabbath, the synagogue ruler said to the people, 'There are six days for work. So come and be healed on those days, not on the Sabbath.' The Lord answered him, 'You hypocrites! Doesn't each of you on the Sabbath untie his ox or donkey from the stall and lead it out to give it water? Then should not this woman, a daughter of Abraham, whom Satan has kept bound for eighteen long years, be set free on the Sabbath day from what bound her?' (Luke 13:11–16)

The woman Jesus saw was demonised. The Greek word used in Luke 13:11 to describe the demonic influence on this woman is *pneuma* (spirit). However, in other places where demonic activity is revealed, such as Mark 1:32 and John 10:21, the Greek word *daimonizomai* is used to describe the condition of the victim. *Daimonizomai* means 'to have a demon'. It can also be translated 'to be pestered', or 'to be possessed' with a demon. Often Christians have been loth to think that they could actually be demonised. To them the word 'demonisation' means 'possession', but in the Scriptures varying degrees of demonisation are recorded, ranging from the example of the woman in the story above to the violently insane demoniac (Matthew 8:28).

To have a demon does not necessarily mean to be possessed by a demon as demoniacs are. The woman above was considered by Jesus to be a woman of faith and so he called her a 'daughter of Abraham' (cf. Romans 4:16). In this case the woman was not possessed, she simply 'had a demon' or was 'pestered by a demon' and so Jesus did not cast out the demon – he simply laid hands upon her and commanded her to be free from her infirmity. I do not believe that a Christian can be possessed in the sense of being indwelt by a demon. But I do believe that like the daughter of Abraham in the passage above, a believer could be 'demonised', meaning he or she is being pestered or physically harassed by a demon.

I remember the testimony of an elderly man during a crusade I held in Ghana in September 1990. He had walked for three miles to get to the crusade on one good leg and one crippled leg aided by a stick. On the second night of the crusade, as I bound and rebuked the spirit of infirmity over the people gathered, he was instantly healed and his bad leg was made whole. He came up onto the platform and gave testimony to the healing power of Jesus.

There is a vast array of spirits of infirmity that seeks to bind people with illness and disease. When we pray for the sick it is important to identify whether a sickness has a spiritual root rather than a physical one. The best guide for this is of course to ask the Holy Spirit.

> The mind of sinful man is death, but the mind controlled by the Spirit is life and peace; the sinful mind is hostile to God. It does not submit to God's law, nor can it do so. (Romans 8:6–7)

The end result of disobedience is a lifestyle that lacks peace, but the obedient see and experience the fruit and power of the Holy Spirit.

(c) *Wrong doctrine.* The aspiration of demons to keep people blind to the truth is not haphazard as some might think. It is manifest across a whole spectrum of activity. One important manifestation is their attempt to lure people into wrong doctrine. This has led to a plethora of strange religions across the face of the earth. Scripture warns that spirits will attempt to introduce false doctrines: 'The Spirit clearly says that in later times some will abandon the faith and follow deceiving spirits and things taught by demons' (1 Timothy 4:1).

As far as the early disciples were concerned, all heresy had its roots in the demonic world. Therefore Christians had every reason to watch their life and doctrine closely, so that they might end up saved and not lost: 'Watch your life and doctrine closely. Persevere in them, because if you do, you will save both yourself and your hearers' (1 Timothy 4:16).

These wrong doctrines have fooled some, causing them to abandon the truth of the gospel. Unfortunately most of these deceived people do not even realise that they have accepted demonic instruction. Not too long ago an attractively charismatic figure named Jim Jones ended up ordering the execution of all his followers. They had all followed him to South America to forge a new life but were destroyed by the man who led them out there. Jones believed up to the end that he was receiving divine instruction. The truth was, he was being deceived by demons.

Even in the Old Testament, where we have only two specific references to demons as such, we find they are mentioned in the context of leading people into worshipping false gods (Deuteronomy 32:17; Psalm 106:36–7). Some individuals in the Old Testament went as far as sacrificing their own sons and daughters to demons. Paul makes it clear that all sacrifices to false gods, whether it is offering pieces of food or the sacrificing of children, are made to demonic powers (1 Corinthians 10:20). The desire of demons is to receive worship; failing that they will cause people to worship something other than God. Adam and Eve were thrown out of the garden because they were convinced by Satan that they could become like God. Satan tempted them to deify themselves and they fell for it. In his appearance Satan took the form of a serpent, one of God's good creations: his intent was to appear in a form acceptable to Adam and Eve.

Demons still attempt to mask their appearance in the process of deception, so that the lies they are passing on may be more acceptable to those they wish to lead astray. Evil spirits take advantage of human stereotypes. For instance, we all have stereotypes of what we consider Satan to look like. One popular image is of a red demon with two horns and a long red fork. Unfortunately he does not make his presence quite so obvious. Such stereotypes have done a lot to undermine a true understanding of how the devil operates.

> And no wonder, for Satan himself masquerades as an angel of light. It is not surprising, then, if his servants masquerade as servants of righteousness. Their end will be what their actions deserve (2 Corinthians 11:14–15)

If we meet a businessman dressed in a smart suit we usually think he is respectable. Our first impression of him encourages us to form a good opinion. We imagine that most people who turn out in a suit are principled, but he may well be steeped in fraudulent practices and illegal dealings. His suit in Western society represents a recognisable symbol of success and respectability: at first glance we would not mind rubbing shoulders with him or even seeking his advice and help in business transactions. But if we found out that he had shady business dealings we would immediately withdraw from contact on a business level.

Scripture makes it clear that Satan takes on the appearance of an angel of light, his intention being to deceive the individual. His works also have the same appearance of acceptability. Satan does not want his work to be seen for what it really is, therefore he masks what he does just as effectively as he cloaks himself. The devil's works often appear to be reasonable and acceptable. Whatever his disguise Satan's goal is to deflect the worship we give to God to someone or something else, if not him directly.

After one meeting I was called over to minister to a young lady. She was confused and explained that she had been involved in satanism and a whole variety of cultic activity. The devil had deceived her into thinking that what she was involved in was all right. She repented of her sin and we began to pray for her, but almost immediately she began to wriggle on the floor like a snake. It was obvious that she was demonised. We broke the power of witchcraft over her life and commanded the bestial spirit to leave her. She was immediately delivered and was able to give praise to God. Though Satan uses deception to take people into varying degrees of doctrinal error, his aim is to drag people into distinct forms of witchcraft. God forbids any involvement in witchcraft:

> Let no-one be found among you who sacrifices his son or daughter in the fire, who practises divination or sorcery, interprets omens, engages in witchcraft, or casts spells, or who is a medium or spiritist or who consults the dead. (Deuteronomy 18:10–11)

One means by which Satan draws people into witchcraft is to get them interested in the future. This is why there are many satanists involved in the art of divination. Horoscopes are just one means the devil uses to influence the way people live. I remember one lady telling me how she was bound by the words spoken to her by a fortune teller. The lady had found that all of the things predicted by the fortune teller had come to pass: she had gone through the tragedy of losing a partner and now thought that she would never marry again. She was completely bound by what had been said to her. Many people around the world have had similar experiences in which a prediction spoken to them has guided and shaped their lives. To be free from the power of such lies there must be repentance.

4. *What deliverance has Jesus won for believers?*

> The Spirit of the Sovereign LORD is on me,
>> because the LORD has anointed me
>> to preach good news to the poor.
> He has sent me to bind up the broken-hearted,
>> to proclaim freedom for the captives
>> and release from darkness for the prisoners,
> to proclaim the year of the Lord's favour
>> and the day of vengeance of our God,
> to comfort all who mourn,
>> and provide for those who grieve in Zion –
> to bestow on them a crown of beauty
>> instead of ashes,
> the oil of gladness
>> instead of mourning,
> and a garment of praise
>> instead of a spirit of despair.
> They will be called oaks of righteousness,
>> a planting of the LORD
>> for the display of his splendour. (Isaiah 61:1–3)

Isaiah had prophesied earlier (9:6ff.) concerning the 'child king' to be born, a ministry which would see the release of the oppressed, as outlined in the above passage from chapter 61. Jesus who came in fulfilment of these two prophecies, announced at the commencement of his ministry that the anointing prophesied by Isaiah was upon him (Luke 4:17–19). Though his aim in coming was to bring about the restoration of fallen humanity to God, this restoration was to include the elimination of every power opposed to humans experiencing a lifestyle of freedom. Just as Jesus does not want us bowing down in worship to other gods he does not want us bound by ungodly forces or any dominating spirit (Matthew 28:18; Mark 16:15–18). Consequently when he came Jesus not only drove out demons but commissioned his disciples to do the same:

> He said to them, 'Go into all the world and preach the good news to all creation. Whoever believes and is baptised will be saved, but whoever does not believe will be condemned. And these signs will accompany those who believe: *In my name they will drive out demons*; they will speak in new tongues; they will pick up snakes with their hands; and when they drink deadly poison, it will not hurt them at all; they will place their hands on sick people, and they will get well.' (Mark 16:15–18, emphasis mine)

In accepting born-again believers as part of his family, God not only gave us a brand new life he also gave us full authority as children to use his name. The Scriptures make it clear that all powers and authorities must bow the knee at the mention of the name of Jesus (Philippians 2:10). Therefore, whenever we come into conflict with demons, and whenever we command them to leave the oppressed, they have to bow their knee. So when operating in the realm of deliverance, it is important to remember and believe that whatever we bind or loose on earth will have already been

bound or loosed in heaven (Matthew 18:16–20), and whenever the people of God come together and agree in prayer,
the Lord will hear and answer. The following points should
be noted.

(a) *Repentance*.   Ministering deliverance is not as difficult a
task as it is sometimes made out to be. The devil no longer
has any jurisdiction over the obedient and repentant children of God. We have been translated out of the kingdom of
darkness into the kingdom of light. In fact the only time the
devil ever gains a place in our lives is when we give him a
foothold (Ephesians 4:27). Suppose a person goes to a
foreign country and commits a crime. That person is subject
to the laws of that country. Similarly Christians who wander
into enemy territory make themselves subject to the power
of the enemy.

If subsequent to becoming a Christian we give the devil
room, then God is willing to rescue us if we repent of our
wrongdoing. Confession is the first step on the road to recov-
ery. When we confess our sins and make ourselves right with
God we can expect him to deliver us. As we obey the word
of God and call upon his name he will rescue us and save us
from evil powers (James 5:16), as everyone who calls upon
his name will be saved (Acts 2:21).

I remember a family who came to a Christian camp at
which I was ministering. They came to listen to one of the
seminars I took on the dangers of the New Age movement.
After the seminar the parents of this particular family told
me an interesting story. They had sent their son Mark to a
'New Age' school when he had been younger. There Mark
had been taught how to open his mind up to external forces

by a technique called 'visualisation', which worked something like this: the child is told to close his or her eyes, and is then told to try to picture things that are not there. For instance a child might be told to imagine that he or she is climbing a set of stairs and that as they get to the top of the stairs they will see an old man sitting on a chair smiling. When the child eventually says they can see such a figure, they may then be asked to listen carefully to what that man is saying. If the child says that the man is speaking, he or she is asked to repeat what is being said. Such teaching methods are demonic and open defenceless children up to demons.

It was not long before Mark began to become allergic to most foods he ate. When he became slightly disturbed, his Christian parents repented of sending him to such a school, but the damage had been done. For about five years Mark suffered severe allergic reactions to most foods. I asked all those present at the seminar to join me in prayer for Mark and took authority over spirits of deception and infirmity, commanding them to leave Mark alone. The next day Mark was completely healed and found himself able to eat eggs, chocolates and various other sweets – things he had not been able to eat for many years without provoking a severe physical reaction.

Repentance means taking responsibility and admitting that we have done wrong. Mark's parents took responsibility for their part in the sin: 'If a person sins and does what is forbidden in any of the Lord's commands, even though he does not know it, he is guilty and will be held *responsible*' (Leviticus 5:17, emphasis mine). Taking responsibility for sin is an important step in the process of being forgiven and healed, or delivered from demonic influences. But repentance is not just a single act; it is a continuous walk in which we live repentant and submissive lives unto the Lord. I have often heard it said that 'you can't crucify demons or cast out the flesh'. Individuals who are unwilling to take responsibility for sin, or repent, cannot have demons cast out of themselves, because their 'will' or 'flesh' is unwilling to be right with God. Though it is possible to cast out demons one cannot cast out the 'will' of a person.

(b) *Self-discipline.* Upon deliverance from evil spirits there has to be a gentle rebuilding of the person's character. New ways of responding have to be learned. Coming to terms with their new-found freedom requires time to adjust. Many will require a lot of reassurance for a few months after they have received deliverance. Self-discipline plays an important part in helping the delivered person walk in the freedom they have obtained. God himself uses discipline to teach and correct his children: 'No *discipline* seems pleasant at the time, but painful. Later on, however, it produces a harvest of righteousness and peace for those who have been trained by it' (Hebrews 12:11, emphasis mine).

A person who has been delivered from a demon of lust may need to give up television. This would be the case if he or she finds it difficult to change the channels when an unsuitable programme comes on. Self-discipline does at times mean doing without and can be quite difficult. The delivered believer needs all the help he or she can get to maintain a godly lifestyle. Such help will be necessary until they have learned how to walk free from old habits and patterns of behaviour through which demons had been able to oppress or keep them in bondage.

(c) *Retaining your deliverance.*   To maintain a repentant and disciplined walk with God the following points are helpful.

1. Maintain a devotional lifestyle that is centred around the word of God. As the psalmist says: 'Great peace have they who love your law, and nothing can make them stumble' (Psalm 119:165; cf. James 1:22–5).
2. Maintain fellowship with other believers who live godly lifestyles.
3. Choose to be fully committed to the will and work of God. Paul commands, 'Honour God with your body' (1 Corinthians 6:20). To maintain freedom from demonic activity a conscious choice has to be made to be completely committed to God's revealed will.
4. Go on being filled with the Holy Spirit (Ephesians 5:18).
5. Develop a lifestyle of praise and prayer (1 Thessalonians 5:16–18). Continuous prayer helps us to maintain sensitivity to the Holy Spirit. A lifestyle of praise ensures that our worship is focused on God rather than on anything or anyone else.

7

Breaking the Sequence of Control

Pulling out the roots

To break the power of the dominator we must recognise two things. First, there is a pattern or cycle of control that will manifest itself (this has been the subject of much of this book). Secondly, there will be roots in the life of the manipulator or dominated individual that will need to be pulled out.

A man who has a weight problem due to compulsive eating might find that he is unable to pass a bakery shop without buying a cream bun. On approaching the counter he may try to convince himself that one bun will not harm him. Usually, at some later stage, such a person will regret his actions and may even be riddled with guilt over the event. The next day, as he walks past the same shop on his way to work, the pattern repeats itself. Once the circle of events has started the compulsive eater ends up buying and eating the cream bun.

Or take the story of Francine, a young, married Christian woman with peculiar behaviour. Her husband Andrew was never allowed to put the children to bed at night. Though this became a point of contention between the couple, Francine never backed down – she always insisted on putting the children to bed. This obsession with the children included a great reluctance to leave Andrew alone with them at any time. Francine consistently arranged her circumstances to ensure that she was always with her children whenever they were not in school.

The case of Mike further illustrates my point. Mike, having moved to a new house and a new job, found that his workmates were reasonably pleasant people. But they constantly ridiculed Jim, one of Mike's workmates. Jim was hurt by the group's insults and wisecracks, and though Jim himself laughed about it, Mike could see that he was being emotionally crushed. Mike found himself in a difficult position: he was afraid of being rejected, but did not want to hurt Jim. However, he began to participate in the derogatory jokes, which were usually at Jim's expense. Later, when he was on his own, he would regret his behaviour, but the next day at work would find him joining in once more.

In each of the three examples above, there is what I would call 'a root problem' responsible for each person's behaviour. It is too easy to label the fictitious character with the weight problem a glutton. But if we found out that he suffered greatly as a child and went to bed most nights without any dinner, our attitude would change. We would then begin to suspect that his overeating problem may not just be the result of a weak will.

When Francine came to me for prayer after a meeting, and

told me the full story behind her fear, her behaviour no longer seemed strange. Francine suffered greatly as a child: she had endured the pain and torture of being abused by her father. Though she was now gloriously born again and married with children, the memories of her past were frighteningly vivid. This was the root of her inability to leave the children alone with Andrew even though he was a born-again believer.

In Mike's case it was obvious that he was without excuse for sinning and needed to repent. But it was not until we discovered that he was put up for adoption by his parents at the age of nine, following a fierce divorce battle, that we finally understood how great his fear of rejection must have been. Before Mike's behaviour could change to one in which the love of Christ was manifest, his fear of rejection had to be dealt with. Having given his life to Jesus he had not been cut off from the rejection he had faced as a young boy. This rejection choked him, causing him to react negatively whenever he faced the possibility of rejection by others. His problems did not manifest with his workmates only. He compromised in any situation if he thought he would be rejected. If the root problems were not dealt with Mike would continue to act in a manner that would ensure acceptance regardless of the consequences to other people.

I once had a terrible toothache and swollen gum and so I went to the dentist. He told me that the pain had been caused because part of the roots of a tooth previously pulled out had been left imbedded in my jaw. It appeared to come out cleanly, but a fragment of the tooth had been left behind. This had become infected and had to be cut out of the gum. It was so badly infected that they had to give me a general anaesthetic to send me to sleep before it could be taken out. But once the root that had caused the infection had been removed I was free from the terrible pain. If the root of a problem is not fully pulled out then it will continue to work under the surface, just like my broken tooth. Before Francine could experience freedom from her phobia the root problem had to be identified, and then dealt with. In Francine's case she had to forgive her father. Once this was done she was released from her irrational fears and was then able to allow Andrew to put the children to bed. When Mike had forgiven his parents his behaviour changed and he was eventually able to stand up to his workmates.

Breaking the power of fear

Fear is the main symptom of all who submit to a controlling influence. An individual could be afraid of exposure, failure, other people, dying, sickness, looking silly, flying, and so on. Each fear can be rooted in a multitude of different events. Just as anger can motivate an individual to react with violence when faced with a threatening situation, fear will usually cause an individual to withdraw when faced with a threat.

The person with a fear of dying could have acquired that fear through watching various horror movies, or perhaps because she visited a spiritist or medium. A person with a fear of failure could have acquired his fear through watching his father reject his other brothers because they failed exams, or he could have acquired the fear as a responsible adult whose boss constantly looked over his shoulder. Whatever the root, fear will be a symptom that motivates behaviour and has to be dealt with at the same time that the roots are being pulled out.

Fear causes us to run away from circumstances, it robs us of the will to face a situation head on and leaves a feeling of dread. In the Bible, the story of Jacob shows him running away from various situations due to fear. The root of his problems lay with his dominating mother. She had told him when and how to deceive his father, and he had obeyed her direction. The fruit of their deception resulted in Jacob rather than his older brother Esau receiving the blessing due to the firstborn. Esau then harboured the desire to kill his younger brother. Jacob consequently fled from home. A number of years later, while on his nomadic travels, he tried to be reconciled to his brother by sending messengers to him, but fear gripped him when he heard that his brother's response was to ride out to meet him with four hundred men. There was nothing that he could do about it. His possessions and his family were too numerous – they could not simply run away. The best Jacob could hope for was that some of his family would escape:

> In great fear and distress Jacob divided the people who were with him into two groups, and the flocks and herds and camels as well. He thought, 'If Esau comes and attacks one group, the group that is left may escape.' (Genesis 32:7–8)

He did not realise that Esau had chosen to forgive and forget his deception. Jacob was still living in a place of fear rooted in his past deceit. Yet, though the eventual meeting with Esau was amicable (Genesis 33:9), it was sad that given the opportunity Jacob did not choose to put things right with

Esau. So the root of the problem between them was not dealt with. The result was that Jacob could not accept Esau's invitation to a place called Seir. Rather, his uncertainty about Esau's motives made him run away once again.

Fear can cause Christians to give in before the battle has been joined. God consistently told his people not to be afraid when in a confrontational situation:

> You will not have to fight this battle. Take up your positions; stand firm and see the deliverance the LORD will give you, O Judah and Jerusalem. Do not be afraid; do not be discouraged. Go out to face them tomorrow, and the LORD will be with you. (2 Chronicles 20:17)

If children of God are willing to confess and put right their past sins God is willing to purify them, not just from their sins but also from the resulting emotional effects of those sins. When, like Jacob, we find ourselves battling with fear arising as a result of our past sin, we need to turn, face the fear and deal with the roots of our sin. To consider what could go wrong is to dwell on the negative. It helps to remember that Jesus is constantly present wherever believers come together to sort out problems. Rather than entertain the fear of what could happen, we need to dispense with the negative and acquire a positive fear of God's ability and power.

I can still recall acquiring my first chicken as a young boy in Nigeria. It was wonderful owning my own chicken. As I did not have a chicken run I made a home for it out of a wooden crate that I stuffed with some straw. Nothing filled me with greater alarm than the thought that it might wander away and end up in someone's cooking pot. To make sure this did not happen I tied one end of a long piece of string to the crate and the other to one of the chicken's legs. I would feed it every morning before I went to school and also when I came back. After a few weeks of keeping my chicken bound in this way, I realised that other relatives who had chickens allowed theirs to roam around. My relatives assured me that if I let mine roam it would come back to its crate to sleep every night. Tentatively, I decided to release it. To my surprise it would not go beyond the area it had been allowed to reach by the rope, and remained like this for two days. On the third day, I determined to have a chicken that roamed as freely as the rest, and so I chased the chicken beyond its previous bounds. To my great delight, I ended up with a chicken that was as great a rambler as any other in our home.

Though not wanting to compare humans to chickens, I do want to bring out a principle here that affects humans just as well as it affected my chicken. I had loosened its bond and released it, yet because it had lived as bound for quite a long time, it continued to behave as bound. Similarly I have found that sometimes after bad roots have been pulled out of a person's life, old fears can cause that person to continue living as before. If not dealt with, the person, though free, will continue to live as if bound.

A heavenly perspective is required to help people see their bonds as broken. This enables them to walk free from the stranglehold that fear tries to generate. In turn this releases people into a workable dimension of faith that receives the word of God and holds on to that word until it becomes their experience. When a person is unafraid (or not worrying, as worry generates fear), they can receive the word of God into their heart and wait patiently for that word to become an experienced reality. Such a person knows that God has spoken and that his word must come to pass. The person who worries has doubted God and has given room for doubt, which is the opposite of faith:

> If any of you lacks wisdom, he should ask God, who gives generously to all without finding fault, and it will be given to him. But when he asks, he must believe and not doubt, because he who doubts is like a wave of the sea, blown and tossed by the wind. That man should not think he will receive anything from the Lord; he is a double-minded man, unstable in all he does. (James 1:5–8)

The person who persists in fear cannot enjoy the promises in the word of God because that person is double minded. People who come to God must believe that he rewards those who earnestly seek him (Hebrews 11:6). In fact fear is expressly forbidden by God:

> So do not fear, for I am with you;
>   do not be dismayed, for I am your God.
> I will strengthen you and help you;
>   I will uphold you with my righteous right hand. (Isaiah 41:10)

The key to unlocking your circumstances

I have heard Christians say things like, 'The very heavens are closed up and I don't seem able to get through.' At times we might feel like the psalmist, thinking that God doesn't seem to answer and that we are without help when we need it the most:

> How long, O Lord? Will you forget me for ever?
> How long will you hide your face from me? (Psalm 13:1)

Yet at the same time we recognise he is our only hope and so we call out to him all the more urgently, but again it seems as if he has deserted us. This I believe is a crucial period in the life of a believer. When a believer is in such a state of mind, they are at their most vulnerable. At this point they are open to the temptation of working out 'the problem' in their own way. It is precisely at this stage that trust in God must not waver.

To be able to stand firm we need to feed ourselves with God's word, which strengthens our faith in the most difficult of circumstances. Jesus' promise is that if we stand firm we will experience his promise of life to the full. Christians who easily give up on God will not find it easy to face the storms of life. The best thing to do in a difficult situation is to cry out to God for help. This is the key to seeing the deliverance of God in every situation:

> The Lord is near to all who call on him,
> to all who call on him in truth. (Psalm 145:18)

God is after the human heart and has proved his willingness to pay the ultimate price by giving his most valued possession, Jesus Christ, who died for us. With that same commitment of love he will allow into our lives anything that will initiate a change of heart when we have strayed from him. He will also use our circumstances to draw us closer to himself.

I remember that even before I became a Christian I would call out to God when I got into trouble. On one particular occasion in Nigeria I remember skipping secondary school so that I could go swimming. I had just turned fifteen and believed that I had somehow attained manhood. On this particular day, in order to prove this point to myself, I decided to indulge in a little drinking at the local swimming-pool bar. With every intention of looking macho I ordered a large drink. The gasp of my friends caused me to puff my chest out just that little bit further. When they also ordered similar quantities of alcohol I decided to go further and ordered the most expensive cigar that the barman could offer and proceeded to inhale every puff I drew from it. After the third large drink I could feel myself turning green and so I decided to make a graceful exit before I fell flat on my face.

The one thing I vividly recall about that day was the way that my distress caused me to call out to God when I got into the privacy of my own room. I was feeling so sick that I thought I was going to die. Consequently I pleaded with God, promising him anything that I could think of if he spared me. The lessons of that day and other similar ones prior to my becoming a Christian have helped me to understand why God sometimes allows difficulties into our lives.

Since becoming a Christian I have found that God continues to allow complications into my life if it will help shape my attitude. I used to find it difficult to be gracious to alcoholics. My attitude towards people with drinking disorders was certainly not as understanding as it should have been. The Lord decided to deal with this in a very ingenious way. I moved house one day to a place that was literally just across the road from my local church. It was wonderful. I then found that once a month a certain elderly gentleman called Phil would arrive at my door drunk. Once he received his monthly pension he would go out on a drinking spree, which would last a few days until he had spent all his money. Every night after each drinking spree he would hire a taxi to take him home, but, once drunk, he could not remember his house number: he was convinced he stayed at number 24 rather than number 42. At first I was irritated, but I eventually became his friend. Repenting of my bad attitude, I would walk him to his house. The friendship grew and I began to develop a godly care for Phil.

Thus it is important to recognise that difficulties are not necessarily a sign of backsliding. God will at times allow problems for some higher reason, which is sometimes not known or easily understood. The Christian's attitude to difficulties has to be filled with faith. He or she is to expect God to deliver every time. Christians are also to expect trouble and persecution because they live and preach the gospel. God will deliver as surely as his enemies will attack. In the middle of the fray, regardless of how it has come, we need to adopt an attitude of heart that refuses to stop seeking God:

> But I call to God,
>   and the LORD saves me.
> Evening, morning and noon
>   I cry out in distress,
>   and he hears my voice.
> He ransoms me unharmed from the battle
>   waged against me,
>   even though many oppose me. (Psalm 55:16–18)

God is in control of all circumstances – he is even in control of time itself. When Jesus heard that his friend Lazarus was sick, the Lord stayed where he was two more days (John

11:6). He was not disturbed by either the sickness or its possible results. Jesus knew that God was in control. Determined not to be motivated by the sickness that was killing Lazarus, Jesus stayed on in the region of the Jordan. We need to get this same kind of faith at work in our own lives, recognising that God works everything out in his own time. We must also acknowledge that he will eventually raise the dead if he has to. Every Christian should copy Jesus, resisting the manipulative threatenings of the devil, or manipulative individuals, regardless of the circumstances.

Restrainer of the dominator

The Bible likens a man without self-control to a defeated city. One whose city walls leave gaping holes enabling enemies to enter at will. Without self-control over his body, soul or spirit, a man will eventually destroy whatever it is he is trying to build: 'Like a city whose walls are broken down is a man who lacks self-control' (Proverbs 25:28).

Esau was hungry and wanted something to eat. Unfortunately he did not consider the price he was paying for the meal he was about to consume. Had he done so, he might not have been so quick to give away his entire birthright. He allowed his hunger to cause him to give up the most important thing he could ever receive from his father: namely, the rights of a firstborn son (Genesis 25:29–34).

In a culture that placed so much value upon birthright it is not enough to say that Esau did not realise what he was doing. Jacob wanted to make sure that there was no going back on the pledge, so he made Esau take an oath. This was to cost Esau dearly. Jacob through deceit eventually received the choicest blessing their father Isaac had to offer, leaving Esau to harbour resentment and murder in his heart against his brother.

Moses' loss of control also cost him dearly. He was a mighty man of God and was usually even tempered, but a couple of times his frustrations let him down. After leading the people of God for over forty years through all kinds of hardships and difficulties, one such outburst of anger locked the door for him into the Promised Land:

> He and Aaron gathered the assembly together in front of the rock and Moses said to them, 'Listen, you rebels, must we bring you water out of this rock?' Then Moses raised his arm and struck the rock twice with his staff. Water gushed out, and the community and their livestock drank. But the LORD said to Moses and Aaron, 'Because you did not trust in me enough to honour me as holy in the sight of the Israelites, you will not bring this community into the land I give them.' (Numbers 20:10–12)

God had told Moses to *speak* to the rock, but instead of doing what he was told Moses *struck* the rock. He was frustrated, the people were grumbling again and this time he lost control. There is a great need in the church today for Christians to be reminded of the spirit of self-control God has given them. Older men are to be examples of the self-controlled – men worthy of respect. This is undoubtedly because we all look up to and imitate our elders. The need for this visible example is not lost on Paul (Titus 2:2). In the end, individuals are responsible for training themselves in righteousness: 'that each of you should learn to control his own body in a way that is holy and honourable' (1 Thessalonians 4:4).

1. *Self-control through the Holy Spirit*

The Holy Spirit works actively in the whole of creation, in accordance with God's will. He is the ultimate controller and his should be the influence we readily respond to. No one can deal with lack of discipline as effectively as the Holy Spirit. Most people who are not sure how to bring their emotional lives under discipline have usually not developed an intimate relationship with the Holy Spirit. We are all individuals driven and motivated by strong emotional forces, however much we may try to deny them. The best way of controlling these is to bring them under the sovereignty of the Spirit of God:

> You, however, are controlled not by the sinful nature but by the Spirit, if the Spirit of God lives in you. And if anyone does not have the Spirit of Christ, he does not belong to Christ. (Romans 8:9)

People sensitive to the Spirit will find that in times of uncertainty they can continue to give themselves over to the Holy Spirit to be led, directed and controlled by him.

2. *Spirit-controlled confrontation of other dominating forces*

When dealing with people trying to exercise domination over ourselves or others, our response must be definite and effective. It is important to come from a place of prayer before we deal with dominators. We must respond spiritually rather than emotionally. What we are confronting is sin in the life of the individual, and not the person. But after prayer we must speak to the manipulator: this is the best way to deal with dominators. Without confrontation most people will just carry on the way they are. Speaking directly to the person will require a response. If we don't tackle the situation head on we are not doing either the controller or ourselves any good.

Spirits also need to be dealt with directly. There is usually no distinction between the spirit and manifestation of its power over the individual. Confrontations in this case take the form of a child of God, given authority by the firstborn of all creation, commanding the spirit to leave in Jesus' name.

In the following appendix we will look at practical ways of facing and confronting the manipulator. I will also give some practical steps to take if we have been manipulating others.

APPENDIX 1

What Next?

Speak to a friend about your situation

1. Choose a neutral friend to whom you will be accountable. Check with your friend and make sure that the problems you are encountering with the manipulator are not arising due to a clash of personalities. If you are a shy person, becoming accountable to someone will help you go through with it. If you are not a shy person, being accountable to a friend will ensure that you deal with the manipulation in a godly manner.
2. Pinpoint the pattern used to control you: think of more than one example of how the other person has manipulated or dominated you. This is important because later on when you face the manipulator that person will want to know when and where he or she has been intimidating you.
3. Pray over the issues with your friend and deal with any areas of fear in your own life.

4. Agree with your friend how you are to arrange an appointment with the manipulator.
5. Book a time to report back to your friend.

Phone, write to or contact in person the manipulator

1. Pray before you phone, write or speak to the manipulator; ask the Lord to reveal his love in your attitude and manner.
2. In your letter or phone call ask if you can meet the other person.
3. Explain that you have a personal problem that you wish to resolve face to face. It is unusual for the manipulator to live too far away to have a face-to-face encounter.
4. If you know you cannot face the other person on your own because he or she is violent, then ask the manipulator if he or she minds the presence of a mutual friend. (Make sure that this is not the same friend to whom you are accountable.)
5. If the manipulator is a member of the opposite sex, take a mutual friend with you. Where possible choose a mutual friend who is the same sex as the manipulator.

At the meeting

1. Open in a time of prayer.
2. Walk in the light: be completely open about the issues. Ask the manipulator to be patient and hear you out completely.
3. Give specific examples of how and when you believe the other person has tried to manipulate, dominate or control you.
4. Conclude with how such manipulation or domination

makes you feel. Then explain that this is why you wanted to see the manipulator.

5. If the meeting is just between you and the manipulator with no one else present and the manipulator denies that he or she has been manipulating, then insist that you should meet again with someone else present. If he or she still says no, quote this passage:

> If your *brother sins* against you, go and show him his fault, just between the two of you. If he listens to you, you have won your *brother* over. But if he will not listen, take one or two others along, so that 'every matter may be established by the testimony of two or three witnesses.' (Matthew 18:15–16, emphasis mine)

6. Unless the manipulator is rebellious or backslidden he or she should concede to the word of God at this point. However, if they refuse to have present an independent arbitrator (an elder) then make it clear that you will not fellowship with them unless there is a change of mind.

If the manipulator accepts that manipulation has taken place

1. Agree to continue in fellowship.
2. Agree that in future you will privately point out things that make you feel manipulated.
3. Close the meeting in prayer.

If demonic activity is suspected

1. Before you go make sure that you are right with God yourself.

2. Insist on taking a mutual friend when you book your appointment to see the manipulator.
3. Consider if fasting and prayer for the manipulator might be appropriate.
4. Having confessed your sins, pray that the blood of Jesus would cleanse you by washing them all away.
5. Take the authority that Christians have been given over evil spirits, telling them to remove themselves from your affairs in the name of Jesus.
6. Proclaim God's word over the plans of the devil, asking God to bring confusion into the devil's plans (Psalm 55:9).
7. Loose the manipulator from the grip of Satan.
8. Spend some time praising God for the victory of Jesus in your life and in the life of the manipulator (if the manipulator is a believer).

If negative information has made you easy to manipulate

1. Repent of accepting and believing the manipulator's lies.
2. Ask a friend to pray with you and break the power of the negative words.
3. Become more disciplined in your reading of the Scriptures. Spend more time confessing the truth of the word of God over your situation.

If this book has helped you to discover what lies at the root of your desire to dominate

1. Ask a friend to pray with you.
2. Admit your sin in prayer.
3. Ask your friend to pray for you.

If you are a dominator in church

1. Have you used your position or wealth to blackmail the leadership?
   - Send a letter of apology to the elders or leaders in the church.
   - Begin to tithe and try to pay back the backdated tithe you have withheld.
   - Offer the leadership assistance to implement the very plans you have been blackmailing them over. Of course this is as long as your conscience accepts that the plans of the leadership are scriptural and not sinful.
   - If you have tried to blackmail the leadership due to your feelings over one individual apologise to the leadership and to that individual.
2. Have you tried to manipulate the church through your spiritual gifts, especially the vocal ones (e.g. prophecy, words of knowledge and tongues)?
   - Repent before God over your misapplication of his gifts.
   - If you know that people have taken action on the strength of your prophecies etc., go and apologise to each one individually.
   - If a whole church has taken action on the strength of your prophecy etc., then write to the leadership and tell them how you feel. Ask them if you could publicly repent to the church as a whole.
3. Have you as a leader attempted to usurp the authority of the other leaders?
   - If you have adopted and encouraged a party spirit, you need to repent to the other leaders in the church

and speak against having allegiances to certain strong individuals.

- If you have publicised confidential information which would force the hand of the rest of the leaders, then you need to humble yourself and apologise to them.
- If you have gossiped about other leaders, you need to consider seriously whether you are called as a leader. If you still believe you are then repent before God at the way you have exposed your fellow leaders.

If you have been dominating in your family

1. Speak to a close friend about your behaviour.
2. Repent in prayer.
3. Agree with your friend how you should approach those you have been manipulating in the family. Also agree how much you should actually say, and to whom you must apologise. It must be remembered that though we are called to walk in the light we are to be careful not to cause a family break-up or quarrel if we can. If you have been a manipulator in the family the most important thing that needs to happen is a change in your behaviour.

Once you have taken any of the steps outlined above, report back to your friend to whom you have chosen to be accountable

1. Continue to pray for the manipulator.
2. Remember to thank God for his help in setting you free from either being a manipulator or being manipulated.

Checklist on Domination

Symptoms of domination

- Do you feel crippled in your witness for Jesus?
- Have you noticed that in certain areas you are unable to attain or maintain a victorious lifestyle?
- Are you experiencing the frustration of having to obey another person even when you know they are wrong and have no authority over you?
- Is there a person who exercises control over you by making a forceful or passive demand?
- Do you feel free or restricted?
- Do you feel crushed or deflated about life?
- Do you have a sense of being bound in a specific situation?

Other people

- Do you feel you are being treated fairly by others?

- Do you feel that strong expectations are being placed on you?
- Are you feeling subdued by another individual?
- Is there a person you cannot talk to about requests they have made?
- Do you have a friend who is very possessive of you?
- Is there a close friend of yours who always appears to be jealous whenever you spend time with other people that they do not get along with themselves?
- Do you have a friend who constantly tries to work things out for you?
- Is there someone who constantly tells you to slow down when you try something new?
- Do you have a spiritual parent that smothers?
- Do you have a spiritual parent that cannot be wrong?
- Is there a person you cannot have a relationship with unless you are subservient?
- Have you received advice that has weighed you down resulting in frustration?
- Have plans been made for you without your consent?
- Do you know a person who always has to take over?
- Do you have problems with someone who does not accept ideas unless they come from him?

Intimidation

- Do you know a person who always gets locked into a battle of wills with you?
- Do you know a person who uses language that is meant to intimidate you?
- Has someone asked you to do something in a manner that has left you with no choice but to say yes?

- Is there a person who threatens to embarrass you by revealing things they know about you?
- Are you afraid to say no to someone in case they become difficult?

Are you a dominator or manipulator?

- Do you have a learned pattern of response in certain situations?
- Do you have a need to direct things for others?
- Are you afraid to allow anyone to organise anything for you?
- Do you expect others to respond to your lead?
- Do you like following the lead of others?
- Do you find it difficult to believe God to intervene and help?
- Do you hear from God before you act?
- Do you trust in God's ability to move on your behalf when you pray?
- Do you find it difficult to delegate?

Where your dependency lies

- Are you dependent upon others more than you are upon God?
- Do you rely on certain methods of doing things?
- Whom do you trust the most in a situation?

Church

- Why do you go to the church you attend?
- Why are you a leader?

- Do you find it easy to accept what your leaders say without complaining?
- What kind of people do you spend your time with?
- Do you find it impossible to lay down your views and opinions?
- Do you criticise because you cannot get your own way?
- Are you devoted to receiving prayer and teaching from the word on a regular basis?
- As a leader what is stopping you from sticking with the vision God gave you?
- As a leader are you afraid to make decisions?
- As a leader have you received financial threats from certain members of the church?
- As a leader do you find that you are afraid to disagree with some members?
- Do you play off individuals or groups against one another?
- As a leader do you take final responsibility for everything under your care?
- Are you preaching a gospel of compromise or out of conviction?
- Do you have a flexible or inflexible attitude about your views?
- Do you find that you have an uncontrollable urge to take the lead in any home-group meeting, even when you have not been asked to do so?
- Do you find it difficult to receive correction from a leader?
- Do you have a driving urge to make the leaders accept the word of prophecy that you bring to a meeting? If it is rejected how do you respond?

- In a prayer meeting is there someone you always feel you have to correct after they pray?

Heavy shepherding

- Have you accepted disciples?
- Do you expect them to take up any advice you give them?
- Is there anyone who has an unhealthy dependency on you?
- Are you giving the Holy Spirit room to convict of sin or do you feel you have to do it?
- Do you hold on to relationships too tightly?

Family and friends

- Do you find it difficult to communicate with your husband or wife?
- When your husband or wife becomes stubborn or disagrees when you feel strongly about something do you threaten him or her in any way?
- Do you withhold attention or intimacy from your husband or wife in an attempt to make them do what you want?
- Has your son or daughter told you or hinted that you are interfering in his or her marriage?
- Are you afraid that your son or daughter will now forget all about you now that they have left home?
- Who is head of the home?
- Who disciplines the children?
- Who is responsible for training the children in the ways of God?

- Are there clear boundaries and responsibilities laid down for the family or do the rules change to suit the head of the home?
- Are you harsh with your husband or wife? If so why?
- Do you honour your parents?
- Do you think your children respect you? If not, how have you tried to win that respect?

Sin and the root of all manipulation

- Is there anyone you are jealous of?
- Is there someone you can't help speaking ill of?
- Are you strongly driven by any desires?
- Do you have any habits you cannot break?
- Are your friends going on with God?
- Do you lose your temper often?